WINDOW SEAT

An aerial perspective of America's forests with general enlightenment for civic leaders

> Frank H. Armstrong
> Department of Forestry
> University of Vermont
>
> Marguerite E. Oates
> Researcher
> South Burlington, Vermont

Bull Run of Vermont, Inc.
7 Deborah Drive
South Burlington, Vermont 05403
Research facilities on Bull Run
of Central Vermont

This book was printed by Queen City Printers Inc. of Burlington, Vermont.

WINDOW SEAT — An aerial perspective of America's forests with general enlightenment for civic leaders.

Copyright © 1988, 1992 by Bull Run of Vermont, Inc. All rights reserved. Printed in the United States of America. Except as permitted under the United States Copyright Act of 1976, no part of this publication may be reproduced or distributed in any form or by any means, or stored in a data base or retrieval system, without prior written permission of the publisher.

Library of Congress Catalog Card Number: 92-138582

ISBN 0-9632448-0-9

CONTENTS

Preface 1
Introduction 2
PART I   AMERICAN FORESTS ENHANCE
         THE QUALITY OF LIFE 6
Chapter
    1. Inter-relationships between forests and our emerging nation . 6
    2. Forestry in other countries of the northern hemisphere 18
    3. The Civilian Conservation Corps (C.C.C.) 33
    4. National Service and attempts to reactivate the CCC 54
    5. Our three conservation eras 62
PART II   AMERICAN TIMBERLAND OWNERSHIP
Chapter
    6. Non-industrial private forests (N.I.P.F.) 72
    7. Forest industry 87
    8. Public forests — government managed 106
PART III   THE EDUCATION OF FORESTERS
Chapter
    9. The education of foresters 118
PART IV   THE WORK OF FORESTERS
Chapter
   10. Wildfire in our forests 123
   11. Forest management and forest inventory 129
   12. Extension, county, consulting, and urban foresters 136
APPENDIX A. Commonly used units of measurement
             & forestry facts 150
APPENDIX B. Reforestation income tax incentive example 154
APPENDIX C. Addresses and glossary of forestry related terms ... 155

TABLES

    1. State percentages of total forest and timberland 3
    2. March 1934 status of the main CCC camps 44
    3. Vermont timberland parcels 250 acres and larger 77
    4. Vermont timberland parcels 100 to 249 acres 78
    5. Small parcels of Vermont timberland transferred 78
    6. State confidentiality on real estate prices 80
    7. Owners of 330 million acres of NIPF 82
    8. The leading seven states in timberland ownership 115
    9. Percent timberland and average growing stock 116
   10. Volume table (extract) 132

TABLES FROM EXTRACTED ARTICLE

    1. Distribution of man-days in Connecticut CCC 49
    5. Analysis of cost per cord in CCC man days 50

ABOUT THE AUTHORS

Frank Armstrong (Ph.D.), commenced a forestry career at a very early age with extended tours of western national parks and national forests. This was in the 1930's conservation era. There followed tours of our southlands, particularly the pine-belts of Louisiana.

The darkening war clouds caused a digression from a forestry career. He enlisted in 1939 at age 17 and was commissioned a lieutenant in 1942. He is a highly-decorated veteran of front-line combat in Europe and Korea with ten combat campaign medals along with other awards for heroism.

He has forestry degrees from West Virginia, Yale, and Duke universities. He has been a timberland owner since 1950. In 1992 he continues to teach numerous sections of American Forestry at the University of Vermont. More than 25% of all baccalaureate degree students are admitted. Many others cannot be accommodated.

Marguerite E. Oates, a Gold-Star widow, worked with the American Red Cross during World War II. She served on the General Staff of the U.S. Army's Infantry School at Fort Benning, Georgia. Marguerite is a Tree Farmer, a writer, and a researcher with some concentration in strategic intelligence.

PREFACE

to *Window Seat (1992 edition)*

This text is used at the University of Vermont for a course entitled "American Forestry". Essentially it is the course which Professor George Henry Perkins commenced in 1878 for future civic leaders. Professor Perkins eventually became the first Dean of the College of Arts and Science at the University of Vermont. The course has a long continuous history with untold numbers of students and about a dozen instructors. Currently more than 25 percent of baccalaureate students enroll in American Forestry during their studies.

This book is directed towards Americans who aspire to be civic leaders, especially in one of our twenty-eight states which are more than 40 percent forested. (You will find those states listed in Table 1.) Legislators, lawyers, bankers, business people, and clergy should understand certain facets of our forests. This book provides the reader with an insight into the reality of that magnificent ocean of green which one sees as they fly over many parts of the United States. There are, and there have been, many people involved in that forest below you. The evidence of pioneers is still there although you can't see it from your window seat. There may have been Civilian Conservation Corps youth down there during the 1930's. It may appear to be one continuous ownership but most likely there are numerous parcels of all sizes. The Forest Service reports there are more than seven million forest ownerships. A typical profile of the current owners will probably provide you with an entirely new viewpoint. It is most pleasant to fantasize into unreality but "unreality is one of the most pivotal social forces shaping our time." (Mitroff & Bennis 1989).

The twelve chapters coincide with the usual fourteen-week semester, allowing one chapter each week plus sufficient time for other matters. The book is only a framework for knowledgeable instructors. Local scenario should be interspersed. We have added field trips with zero travel time by producing twelve video recordings with the instructor interviewing foresters on location. We have added numerous 35 mm slides, some of which are photo-prize winners. They were donated by people across the nation. We include one species of tree in each session, a species which is connected with the overall theme for that week. For example, chapter 1 includes white pine, chapter 2 includes larch, and chapter 5 Norway spruce.

Our cover photo, showing racial diversity in the C.C.C., is from the files of the American Forestry Association.

LITERATURE CITED

Mitroff, Ian I. and Warren Bennis. 1989. *The Unreality Industry* A Birch Lane Press Book.

WINDOW SEAT

An aerial perspective of America's forests with general enlightenment for civic leaders
by Frank Armstrong and Marguerite Oates

INTRODUCTION

About one-third of the United States is forest but our forests are so concentrated that if you have a window seat flying over the east, the west coast, or Alaska the probability is that you are over forest. The two subsets of forests are timberland and non-commercial forest. Timberland is that forest which is capable of producing commercial crops of wood and which has not been reserved from timbering by law or statute. In earlier publications timberland was called "commercial forest". Some writers refer to timberland as "productive forest". In Europe the term "high forest" has much the same meaning. Non-commercial forest, on the other hand, includes high elevation forests, very northern latitude forests in Alaska, our designated wilderness areas, and of course New York State's Adirondack Park which in accord with the state constitution will remain forever wild. Some writers differentiate non-commercial forest into "reserved forests" meaning designated wilderness areas and "woodlands" referring to the non-productive forest. This non-productive forest is called "low forest" in Europe.

If you are viewing Maine, New Hampshire, West Virginia, or Vermont from your window seat you are in all probability over timberland (Table 1). In the eastern states most of the forest is classified as timberland. As more wilderness areas are designated the extent of timberlands will decrease. The percentage of the total terrain in forest has been increasing in recent years in many states. Massachusetts, for example, increased their percentage of forest by 6.0 percent from 1972 to 1985 (Dickson 1987). The Forest Service has also reported recent increases in the extent of forests in at least Ohio, Pennsylvania, Maryland, Missouri, New Hampshire, Vermont and West Virginia. Missouri's increase in forest acreage was 26 percent in a 17-year period.

The United States Forest Service estimates that forest acreage throughout the United States will decrease at about eight hundredths of one percent for each of the next fifty years (Haynes 1988). Essentially this is an insignificant decrease.

This book is written for Americans who are, or may become, civic leaders. Table 1 illustrates the relative importance of timberland to the economy of many states in which you may make your career. Governors and other leaders of these states should have some idea of what forests do for people; who owns our forests and why; prices being paid for forest property; the extent of forest property transfers; and the role of foresters. We will not delve into matters any deeper than is necessary to accomplish our objective.

Table 1 STATE PERCENTAGES OF TOTAL FOREST AND TIMBERLAND RANKED BY PERCENTAGE OF TIMBERLAND (Bones 1989)

State	Percent in Forest	Percent in Timberland	Nat. Forest	Nat. Park	F&WL Refuge	For. Cnslt	State Tree
Maine	89.8	87.0	#	#	#	156	E.W. pine
New Hampshire	88.1	84.2	#		#	132	Pa. birch
West Virginia	77.5	76.6	#			35	Sug. Maple
Vermont	75.7	74.8	#		#	63	Sug. Maple
Alabama	66.9	66.7	#		#	355	Sou. pine
South Carolina	64.3	63.8	#		#	115	Cabb. Palm.
Georgia	64.9	63.5	#		#	146	live oak
Virginia	63.2	61.1	#		#	89	dogwood
Massachusetts	62.0	60.3			#	163	Am. elm
North Carolina	61.0	59.2	#	#	#	96	pine
Connecticut	58.7	57.5			#	13	Wh. Oak
Pennsylvania	59.4	56.6	#		#	117	E. hemlock
Mississippi	55.3	55.3	#		#	169	Sou. Magn.
Rhode Island	59.8	55.2				5	red maple
New York	62.0	52.2			#	95	Sug. maple
Arkansas	51.0	50.0	#	#	#	42	pine
Tennessee	50.3	48.7	#		#	30	Yell. Poplar
Louisiana	48.7	48.7	#		#	74	bald Cyp.
Michigan	50.1	47.8	#		#	94	E.W. pine
Kentucky	48.4	47.0	#	#		19	Ky. Coffeet.
Florida	48.4	44.1	#	#	#	46	Cab. Palm.
Wisconsin	44.1	42.4	#		#	102	Sug. maple
New Jersey	42.7	41.2			#	45	N. red oak
Washington	51.4	39.7	#	#	#	92	W. hemlock
Maryland	41.8	39.1			#	37	W. oak
Oregon	45.6	35.9	#	#	#	166	Doug. fir
Delaware	33.0	32.2			#	4	Am. holly
Idaho	41.4	27.6	#		#	48	W.W. pine
Missouri	28.4	27.2	#		#	29	Fl. dogwood
Ohio	27.9	27.2	#		#	27	OH. buckeye
Minnesota	32.7	26.8	#		#	40	red pine
Indiana	19.4	18.8	#		#	37	Yell. poplar
Colorado	32.2	17.7	#	#	#	32	blue spruce
Hawaii	42.5	17.0			#	5	kukui
California	39.5	16.8	#	#	#	439	redwood
Montana	23.6	15.9	#		#	24	Pond. pine
Illinois	12.0	11.3	#		#	11	W. oak
Oklahoma	16.6	10.8	#		#	17	E. redbud
Texas	8.1	7.4	#	#	#	66	pecan
Wyoming	16.1	7.0	#	#	#	3	cottonwood
New Mexico	23.9	6.7	#	#	#	3	pinyon
Utah	30.9	5.9	#	#	#	4	blue spruce
Arizona	26.7	5.2	#	#	#	7	paloverde
Alaska	35.7	4.4	#	#	#	16	Sitka Sp.
Iowa	4.4	4.1			#	4	oak
South Dakota	3.5	3.0	#	#	#	6	white spr.
Kansas	2.6	2.3			#	8	cottonwood
Nebraska	1.5	1.1	#		#	6	cottonwood
North Dakota	1.0	0.8		#	#	8	Am. elm
Nevada	12.7	0.3	#		#	5	S.L. pinyon

Much of America's eastern primeval forest was cleared for agricultural purposes. The remaining forest was, by and large, cutover by the early lumbermen. But, we are not criticizing them for we believe as Austin Cary did.

> "It has been rather fashionable of late, particularly in the field of conservation, to condemn everything that is past. Maine foresters, far as I know, have not joined in that. We honor our ancestors, who in the hard conditions of pioneer life used these woods as they might for the sustenance and comfort of their families, and later lumbermen as well, who on the basis of the natural resource built up prosperity here. Sensible men, we call them, for that; nor do we see reason to attribute to them a reckless and wasteful spirit." (Cary 1935).

Austin Cary, our first industrial forester, was speaking with the New England Section of the Society of American Foresters at Mooslookmagentic House in Rangeley, Maine.

After the Civil War people became concerned about our forest depletion. This book will tell you of the action they took to restore our forests. Certainly Mother Nature cooperated. There were decades when a forthcoming timber famine was clearly on the horizon. But then in 1983 it was abruptly recognized that if there was any timber supply problem in America in the 1980's it was simply that we had too much wood. The one century of American forestry is one of the greatest success stories ever told. This book will tell you about the dedication of many people who restored our forests. Most important, it will inform you about ownership of that ocean of green trees that you view from your window seat.

The best evidence of the success of American forestry in dealing with the timber famine, which had been predicted since the 1890's, is the commodity market. Lumber futures were first traded in 1968. The price per thousand board feet (m.b.f.) of the standard grade has stabilized despite the double-digit inflation era we experienced in the late 1970's. In early 1991 lumber future prices range between $190 and $220 per m.b.f. Prices for lumber are very volatile and have ranged from a low of $100 in late 1974 to $285 in late 1979. There were also peaks of $250 in 1982; $225 in 1987; and $195 in 1973. These are current dollars, not corrected for inflation. Lumber prices converge with lumber future future prices as the futures mature. Prices for standing sawtimber also stabilized in the 1980's. Mississippi prices averaged $180 per m.b.f in 1980; $150 in 1985 and 1986; and $180 in 1989. Pulpwood prices, in Mississippi, followed a similar pattern.

LITERATURE CITED

Armstrong, Frank H. 1990. Forestry instruction for civic leaders of the 21st Century. Journal of Forestry Vol. 88, No. 1.

Bones, James T., Branch Chief for Forest Inventory and Analysis Research, USDA, Forest Service. Personal correspondence October 10, 1989.

Cary, Austin. 1935. Forty years of forest use in Maine. Journal of Forestry Vol. 33, No. 4; 366-372.

Dickson, David R. & Carol L McAfee. 1987. Forest statistics for Massachusetts 1972 and 1985. Resource Bulletin NE-106. USDA Forest Service.

Haynes, Richard W. 1989. An analysis of the timber situation in the United States: 1989-2040. Part II: The future resource situation (draft). USDA Forest Service.

WINDOW SEAT

PART I AMERICAN FORESTS ENHANCE THE QUALITY OF LIFE

Chapters 1, 2, 3, 4, and 5 are essentially case histories with evidence of how owning, working in, and recreating in American forests have enhanced the lives of untold numbers of people. It is one thing to look at a forest, from a distance or close up. It is quite another thing to have a justifiable reason to be there, a sense of purpose. Some people, including farmers, feel a sense of greater accomplishment knowing they are in the production sector of our economy. Tree farmers and many timberland owners are in the production sector.

CHAPTER 1 INTER-RELATIONSHIPS BETWEEN FORESTS AND OUR EMERGING NATION

Our forests are a changing community subject to periodic setbacks in what would otherwise be a smooth succession of timber types concluding in a climax forest. The last glacier, which covered much of the United States with hundreds of feet of ice, withdrew 14,000 years ago. For the next three thousand years much of northern United States was covered by tundra. Then slowly aspen, and some pine trees spread into the northeastern region from the south. Aspen, in particular, is known as a pioneer species. It is frequently the first species of tree to grow back into areas following any clearing. Then other tree species slowly encroach into the area. These include white pine, ash, and paper birch in the northeast. Timber types vary in different regions. Eventually the climax species becomes established (hemlock, sugar maple, American beech along with other species in much of the northeast). These are the very durable species which can survive in the shade of other trees until they are free to grow. They generally live for hundreds of years. The climax forest type is capable of continuing to hold the ground forever barring any setbacks. The northeastern forest primeval was generally the climax timber type.

Forests, throughout the world, continue to be subject to setbacks of their ecological succession from wildfire, storms, volcanoes, and agricultural clearing. The widespread use of fire by Native Americans was documented by early expeditions including the Lewis and Clark Expedition of 1805 (DeVoto 1953: 222). In 1979 the elderly descendants of Native Americans and homesteaders were interviewed to establish the reasons why Native Americans had purposely set fires (Barrett 1979). Most fires were set to achieve multiple objectives which included

1. Burn out the old, dense underbrush to stimulate a new growth of big-game browse.
2. Protect the forest from destructive crown fires by reducing fuel accumulations.

3. Enhance the growth of food plants such as berries.
4. Facilitate travel through the forest.
5. Improve forage for horses (after 1700 when native Americans had acquired horses).
6. Kill insects and tree diseases.

Some of the reasons are the same that are cited by today's foresters for the use of controlled burning and for permitting some lightning-instigated fires to burn.

The pioneers may have found a climax forest in some regions, such as northern New England, but in other regions they found a forest that was in transition towards a climax forest. The pioneers avidly set about clearing the forest in order to establish their family farms. Felling of large trees with a broad axe was arduous work. Crosscut saws were not used until about 1890. Large white pine was prized for ship masts, much of which was exported to Europe. Certain species of oak were used for wooden-ship hulls. Some wood from the cleared trees was used for construction, but most was burned or made into charcoal. Iron and steel production required charcoal. Steam ships were fueled by wood and also built from wood. Railroads were fueled by wood, the trains ran on wooden cross ties and over many wooden trestles. Wood ash was slaked and made into potash. It was the first cash crop for many pioneers. Plank roads spanned muddy terrain. Large volumes of wood were shipped to the West Indies and Europe (Perlin 1989). More than three fourths of Vermont was cleared for farming by 1850. Today more than three fourths of Vermont is in forest. The story of this clearing followed by reversion to forest is our topic for this chapter.

Large trees draw as much as 80 gallons of water per day from the soil and transpire it into the atmosphere. Thus forest clearing resulted in more runoff water in creeks during wet periods. Hence water powered saw mills were feasible in that era. Today the same sites don't have the water surges because of the trees. However, forests conserve moisture and can humidify regions (Giono, Jean).

A hike through most any eastern forest will reveal long-abandoned stone walls, cellar holes, wire fences, and cemeteries which just cannot be seen from your window seat. These are evidence of our land-use history. The frontiersmen left the relative comforts of civilization and forged a new life on the frontier. Many of these pioneers vanished in our forests leaving a stone cellar hole, and a few stones arranged to encircle their spring; the resting place for their bones is often not marked; and these secrets are known only to the trees. Was this agricultural clearing for a mere century of farming all in vain? Or were these the acts that strengthened our nation?

If you select a parcel of timberland, particularly in the east, and establish the land-use history you probably have a case history which parallels this report. You can use land records, census reports, birth and death records, and discussions with old timers.

Most of the United States was the frontier at one time. Pioneers aspired to complete freedom, including economic independence. They developed self-reliance, fortitude, and compassion for the less fortunate. A great deal of hard labor was expended by the pioneers and their children in clearing the farm, pulling out stumps, building the home and barn, constructing stone walls and split-rail fences, along with the usual subsistence farm operations. Life was short and hard. Nevertheless, it was the nature-oriented life-style they wanted. A tour of most any old cemetery is clear evidence of the adversity families underwent.

The Moravian Church Colony in North Carolina appointed a "Forester and Superintendant of Hunters" in 1759. Philip Christian Gottlieb Reuter, (born in Steinbach, Germany in 1717) came to America with his surveyor's certificate. Reuter saw to the wise use of the church-owned forests which were leased to members of the church (Doggett 1987). The forest inspector was charged with watching for trespassers trying to exploit the hunting.

Thomas Cole was idealizing the American wilderness in his landscapes by 1829. He is recognized as the originator of the Hudson River, or American School, of landscape painting. He gave landscapes spiritual meaning that he had acquired from nature. Cole imbued American wilderness with a new found authentic and moral responsibility. Thomas Cole realized he must begin as nature does, seeking the principle at the heart of the scene and then move outward and upward. This was in sharp contrast with European artists who viewed forests as a barrier to civilization, a tangled maze, a moral wilderness.

> Thomas Cole was the father of American landscape painting; The right man in the right place at the right time; the first to make the recording (and expressive interpretation) of American wilderness his major theme. Cole believed the object of painting was not merely to please, but to exalt, and enoble (Merritt 1969).

In Cole's "View of the White Mountains" a young flourishing elm tree surges upward through a dead tree. Elm trees, in particular, connotate America for there were several famous elm trees associated with early American history. These include the Penn Treaty Elm, the Liberty Tree of Boston, and the Washington Elm. Cole's painting depicts harmony with people. Purity is exemplified by the dark foreground, the radiant Mt. Washington, and the prominent broad path with people. Mt. Washington is a name synonymous with the highest virtue.

Cole made sketches in the field but painted in a studio. He frequently used dead trees to denote the transience of life. Waterfalls give a voice to some of his landscapes. Tree stumps indicated progress but at a cost. (McGrath 1989). Cole was also deep into poetry and music.

Cole's acquaintance, J. Fennimore Cooper, also keenly influenced by American wilderness, was idealizing magnificent landscapes of America in prose. "His early novels taught Europe more about America than Europe had ever learned before" (Clymer 1900). J. Fennimore Cooper in *Leather-Stocking*, for example, portrayed the pioneer as an unsophisticated homespun American whose finest characteristics came from contacts with forest wilderness. The Reverend Jeremy Belknap, founder of the Massachusetts Historical Society, had excelled in his earlier satirical allegorical account of colonial settlements in his book *The Foresters* (Clymer 1900) and (Belknap 1796).

By the Civil War era clearing of the eastern forests for agricultural uses had reached a high point. After the war many returning veterans, having travelled to distant lands and having realized opportunities, migrated west. Their elderly parents carried on farming as long as possible, but slowly fields were abandoned and reverted to forests. Pioneer tree species which invaded abandoned pastures and meadows varied in different regions. However, in New England conditions were frequently ideal for white pine. It grows very slowly for about five years and then, if it is free to grow and not overtopped by hardwoods, it becomes the fastest growing tree in the woods. Hence the abandoned fields were ideal for seeding by the few remaining white pine seed trees which were scattered over the terrain. The ensuing old-field white pine stands grew to sawtimber size in 50 years.

The natural range of eastern white pine is from the Maritime provinces of Canada, south to northern Georgia along the Appalachian Mountains, and west to Minnesota. Stands of amazingly large white pine can be found in the Appalachian mountains.

Eastern white pine can be readily identified because there are five needles to a cluster. White pine is frequently obvious from a distance with a silhouette that is broad and not conical at all. It can reach heights not approached by the other species which associate with it. White pine is an evergreen but each autumn about one third of the needles turn brown and fall to the forest floor.

The American Forestry Association has maintained a register of the nation's largest trees for about fifty years. The champion tree of each species is selected by a formula that includes total height, crown spread, and trunk diameter. The national champion eastern white pine is in Michigan with height of 158 feet and diameter of 17 feet. There are taller white pines, but they don't have the diameter.

If white pine is free to grow after about a five-year establishment period it can grow three to four feet per year. Growth of pine trees is obvious because each year they produce a leader growth tipped by a bud. The next year, while a new leader is soaring upwards, the bud expands into a whorl of branches and so you can count the internode spaces and determine the age of a pine tree.

The pathological longevity of eastern white pine is about 160 years. Thence it generally commences to be set back by decay problems. They have been known to live as long as 400 years.

The pine cones take two years to mature, producing a good seed crop every three to five years. The wind dispersed seed can travel more than 500 feet.

Native Americans used white pine inner bark for healing wounds and for cough remedies. The wood is light, resilient, and strong enough to be used for construction. Formerly it was widely used for ship masts and spars. Now it is used for construction, panelling, cabinets, and furniture.

The time frame varied for the abandonment of agricultural lands. Although many northeastern fields were abandoned in the 1870's, others were abandoned in the 1920's or even 1930's. Lumbermen commenced logging the Lake States about the Civil War era and then moved west and south. The American frontier line was all the time shifting westward until 1890 when the Bureau of the Census announced the distinct American frontier line no longer existed. But it was in those years, immediately following the Civil War, that the huge migration westward became a stampede. New towns, cities and railroads (all voracious users of wood) sprang up like asparagus in April.

Americans reacted to the situation and our first great conservation movement, known as the Great Crusade, commenced. But this one story is so very important to us that we will hold it for chapter five.

Pioneers were primarily interested in sustenance of their families. They fully appreciated the amenity values of the American wilderness, along with their expanding farms. They were practical, inventive people who made wide use of expedients. Individualism, fortitude, restlessness, and exuberance dominated the scene. Freedom, including economic freedom, was the name of the game.

Our finest historians have written on this interaction between our forest frontiers and American people. I intend to cite a few of their writings, with the hope that this may inspire you to delve more deeply into our land-use history. Foremost is the writing of Frederick Jackson Turner. Most any library will have his writings as well as those of his critics and defenders. Benjamin F. Wright, Jr., professor of political science at Harvard and President of Smith College, stated "The most brilliant and the most influential of American historians, Turner has colored all of our thinking about the growth of the American Nation" (Taylor 1971). Avery Craven, who enjoyed a long and distinguished career at the University of Chicago, stated "Frederick Jackson Turner wrote less and influenced his own generation more than any other important historian" (Taylor 1971). Walter Prescott Webb spent most of his life as professor of history at the University of Texas. He also acknowledges the dominance of Turner's writing. "That paper made Frederick Turner a scholar with honor in his own country; it altered the whole course of American Historical writing ever done in the United States" (Taylor 1971).

"Frederick Jackson Turner has stated the undeniable fact — that an organic connection exists between American democracy and the American

Frontier (Elkins and McKitrick 1954). "Turner used the word 'frontier' in loose fashion. Sometimes it referred to a place where men were scarce and nature abundant (Taylor 1971). Some excerpts from the Turner Thesis of 1893 (Turner 1920):

> The policy of the United States in dealing with its lands is in sharp contrast with the European system of scientific administration. Efforts to make this domain a source of revenue, and to withhold it from immmigrants in order that settlement might be compact, were in vain.... The frontier individualism has from the beginning promoted democracy.. The result is that to the frontier the American intellect owes its striking characteristics. That coarseness and strength combined with acuteness and inquisitiveness; that practical, inventive turn of mind, quick to find expedients; that masterful grasp of material things, lacking in the artistic but powerful to effect great ends; that restless, nervous energy; that dominant individualism, working for good and for evil, and withal that buoyancy and exuberance which comes with freedom — these are the traits of the frontier.. America has become another name for opportunity...

In a later paper entitled "Contributions of the West to American Democracy" Turner wrote:

> Western democracy through the whole of its earlier period tended to the production of a society of which the most distinctive fact was the freedom of the individual to rise under conditions of social mobility, and whose ambition was the liberty and well-being of the masses. This conception has vitalized all American democracy, and has brought it into sharp contrasts with the democracies of history, and with those modern efforts of Europe to create an artificial democratic order by legislation.

In commenting on the Turner thesis, Benjamin F. Wright, Jr. (Fox 1934) stated:

> American democracy was born of no theorist's dream; it was not carried in the Susan Constant to Virginia nor in the Mayflower to Plymouth. It came out of the American forest, and it gained new strength each time it touched a new frontier.

Roy M. Robbins (Robbins 1962) states:

> As Professor Turner has so ably demonstrated, the victory of Jackson meant that an agricultural society, strongest in the regions of rural isolation rather than in the areas of greater density of population and of greater wealth, has triumphed for the moment over the conservative, industrial, commercial, and manufacturing society of the New England type. It meant that a new, aggressive, expansive democracy, emphasizing human rights and individualism, as against the old established order which emphasized vested rights and corporate action, had come into control. For the first time in world history, a frontier society came into control of national policy Senator

Benton of Missouri exclaimed "The manufacturers want poor people to do the work for small wages; these poor people wish to go to the West and get land; to have flocks and herds — to have their own fields, orchards, gardens, and meadows — their own cribs, barns and dairies, and to start their children on a theatre where they can contend with equal chances for the honors and dignities of the country.

The foregoing was the scenario (1837) when Horace Greeley, editor and joint owner of The New Yorker, advised laborers to go to the Great West in view of the economic panic of that year. In 1849 Greeley declared the soil was God's gift to man. The 1856 platform of the Republican Party included the Homestead Plank as written by Horace Greeley. The Homestead Act was signed by President Lincoln in 1862 (Robbins 1971).

The American frontier ceased to exist in 1890 according to the Bureau of the Census. And this report was probably the instigation of the Turner Thesis. The westward youth migration to the new frontier, particularly of youth who had developed a superb work ethic, provided the new lands with superb civic leaders. Leading citizens, in county after county, were people with no previous political experience. The new states had true citizen legislatures.

Two of every five Vermonters left the state between 1850 and 1900....
They went everywhere in the expanding nation Most remarkable are the many who prospered and became leaders of the rising West and the Burgeoning cities. Being Vermonters most of them knew how to work hard, and they were shrewd, practical, and enterprising.
... Eight of the first eighteen Wisconsin governors were Vermonters...There were 88 Vermonters in Congress between 1850 and 1900 representing 18 other states... The University of Vermont produced ten Congressmen from the classes of 1837 to 1843 out of 142 degree recipients. (Morrissey 1981).

Much of the hard work Morrissey cites was forest oriented. The interaction between forests and people continues to strengthen our Republic. These values are intangible and defy economic computerization. They, nevertheless, are very real.

The forest frontier shaped the American pioneer as much as the American pioneer shaped the forest. The pioneers shed their European heritage and established a new identity. Immigrants were Americanized.

Old-field white pine generally grew very well on abandoned meadows and pastures which had been grazed for decades. Erosion and soil nutrient depletion seemed to give way to forest resiliency. As the white pine became saw log size hardwood regeneration developed under the pine. These hardwoods were tolerant of the shade of the pines and although they did not grow very fast they survived and waited for the pine to be felled. Small sawmills, many of them steam powered, sprang up in the white pine areas and much of the pine was sawn into low grade lumber. The low grade was no problem because the dominant use of this wood was for box boards. Cardboard boxes did not come into general use until after World War I.

Forestry in World War I included four important topics which will be discussed in later chapters. There was the AEF 20th Forestry Regiment, the Spruce Production Division, the IWW, and timber research in kiln drying.

If you had a train window seat travelling through eastern United States in 1936 you would have seen millions of acres of saplings along with endless cotton fields in the South. Sawtimber was still not scarce because there were the western forests, the south central forests, and ample eastern forests of old-field white pine, hardwoods, vast stands of spruce in Maine, and our southern pines. The U. S. Forest Service continued to predict a timber famine as they had been doing since 1905.

In 1930 a generous friend of the Harvard Forest, and Professor Richard T. Fisher, first director of the Forest planned a forestry museum on the Forest at Petersham, Massachusetts. The principal features were a series of small scale models illustrating local land-use history. Nearly 500 artist-months were devoted to the 24 models. The typical case history we are discussing parallels this display. Brochures and slides are available from Harvard Forest, Petersham, Massachusetts (Cline 1936).

The Civilian Conservation Corps was established in 1933. This is such an important topic that Chapter 3 will be relegated to that topic.

World War II was fought with wood. "The war machine was fed with lumber, chiefly by denying it to civilians" (Greeley 1951). Wartime demand for wood consumed 215,000,000,000 board feet in six years. This was the equivalent of 20 million homes. It was ten million acres of timber. This wood from American forests was used as follows:

(NOTE: MBF means thousand board feet, MMBF means millions of board feet, and MMMBF means billions of board feet.)

48 MMMBF for construction of cantonements, factories, and shipyards.

43 MMMBF for truck bodies, ammo boxes, and packing & crating. Truck bodies required 1 MMBF per day (ash and oak). Many of the trucks, and other wood products, were shipped to the USSR and our other allies.

10 MMMBF for weapons, airplanes, patrol boats, and ship parts.

There were many specialty uses. Foresters scoured South America for balsam wood for floats and life rafts. American biologists scoured South America for quinine bark to be used for Malaria medicine. Mahogany was needed for PT boats. Airplane propellers were made from yellow birch in the early days of the War. Cork was made from Douglas fir bark rather than the usual Mediterranean cork oak. Wilson Compton of the National Lumber Manufacturers stated "Wood has become the great substitute for substitutes" (Compton 1942). It was not possible to buy lumber without a war production board permit. No softwood lumber was available to the public. Foresters, loggers, sawmill men etc. were exempt from the draft but many joined the military anyway. Forestry schools trained military specialists. Japanese incendiary balloons aggravated the western forest fire problem at a time when the Civilian Conservation Corps was being ended. California initiated a program which is carried on till this day of using correction center inmates for forest fire control.

Lumbermen had a multitude of unusual problems. Gasoline was rationed, but for lumbering exceptions could be made. Tires were nearly impossible to procure. Logging cables, tractors, saw blades etc. had to continually undergo improvised repairs. There was difficulty obtaining enough meat for the logging crews to provide sufficient calories for the hard work.

There were three important developments for forest products industry during the war.
1. Wider diversification of the uses of lumber and timber products and wood treatments.
2. Development of modern timber engineering and timber fasteners.
3. Great advances in the gluing field, plywood and laminated wood.

Capital gains treatment of timberland earnings was approved by Congress in 1943. It meant that revenue from timberland was taxed at a lower rate than normal income. Forest products corporations realized that earnings from growing timber were taxed at a lower rate than was paid by their sawmill, the papermill or other manufacturing. This caused great intensification of woodland operations, and significantly contributed to the excellent situation we have today. The 1986 income tax reform revoked this incentive. Possibly the incentive will be restored in the 1990's.

When World War II ended the Forest Service felt that timberlands would be severely overcut because of the pent-up demand for lumber. They advocated federal government control of forest management on privately-owned forests. The objective was to increase wood production of our forests. There was much resistance to the idea and the program was never implemented. Congressional moves to give returning veterans Alaskan land were defeated.

There was a tremendous backlog of demand for wood when the war ended. Virtually all economists predicted a nation-wide economic recession. They were wrong, and there was ten years of prosperity along with unparalleled demand for wood throughout the world. It trebled stumpage values (the value of standing timber trees) and gave timber growing an economic footing it never had before. Thus World War II ushered in the golden age of American Forestry. It is too bad that it took a war to do it. The increased stumpage prices, caused by the pent-up demand for wood, instead of depleting the forest resource intensified forest management resulting in our abundant wood supply of today.

By 1950 the saplings of the 1930 era had become pole-sized timber, meaning diameters of about 12 inches. Mortality amongst saplings was such that the number of stems per acre was reduced from about 2,000 or more down to about 300. Tree mortality, as stands progress from the sapling stage, can be very high. The federal Soil Bank program was a strong incentive to plant many worn-out southern cottonfields to fast growing loblolly and slash pine. This was a highly successful program.

By 1980 pole stands of the 1950 era had reached sawtimber size. Trees from the Soil Bank program were pulpwood and small sawtimber sized. The CCC planted trees were sawtimber sized. Forest industry's intensification of forest management, in response to the capital gains treatment of timberland earnings, was paying off. And the hard work of the Great Crusade had reached fruition. Timber supply was tantamount to an underwater tidal wave which no one viewed until it crashed on shore. For example, between 1972 and 1989 the sawtimber growing stock on the Mark Twain National Forest (Missouri) increased 53 percent. And, even this startling performance was exceeded by the state of West Virginia which had a 60 percent increase in sawtimber growing stock between 1975 and 1983. Thus the threatening timber famine vanished in the early 1980's. Prices for standing timber, and lumber, have stabilized as result of the success of American forestry.

Annual consumption of wood products, in the United States, was shattering all previous records by 1987. And yet, in the 1980's we were growing far more wood than we were cutting. For one example, a recent study revealed that Pennsylvania could increase their annual cut of hardwood by 20-fold and still be within sustained yield allowable cut (Gansner et al 1987). Even if the Canadians stopped sending us most of their production we could continue our current level of consumption under sustained yield. In each recent year forest industry and non-industrial private forest owners have been planting nearly two billion trees, despite economic dis-incentives that are discussed in Chapter 5. This is more than the CCC planted in nine years. The National Tree Trust (a federal program) also plans to plant another two billion trees per year in the 1990's. However, none have been planted under this program as of December 1991.

The specter of a timber famine has vanished from the horizon for the moment. Wood on the market is surplus to our needs. However, there are Forest Service predictions that demand for wood may double or treble by the year 2040 (Haynes 1989).

Beneficial interaction between forests and people has continued through the present. We possess millions of acres of public forests (government managed) which are available to everyone. Even more meaningful is the opportunity for most Americans to own their personal forest. Fortunately many Americans don't aspire to own a forest; those who do, generally experience a short period of ownership; the demand is so low that prices for forest properties remain modest; and as we will see in chapter six, even persons with modest incomes manage forest ownership; and wealthy persons seem to aspire to own intangible property rather than real estate. This latter statement could be inverted, for once I heard it said that wealthy persons are wealthy because they did not invest in forest properties.

Forests have played a vital role in American history. An understanding of this history is the basis for a full appreciation of the potential to be derived from fostering a continuing interaction between forests and people. At this very moment there are Americans coping with the challenges of wilderness conditions and becoming stronger, physically and mentally because of their experience. There are loggers who are becoming more self-reliant because of the physically challenging way of life. And there are families who, while at hunting or fishing camp, are forging closer family ties.

Thomas Cole and J. Fennimore Cooper declared in landscapes and novels "The west was spiritually pure, superior to a decadent Europe. While the broad axe and the plough might subdue it, the experience of being in it would purify human society, a theme Frederick Jackson Turner would later take as the guiding principle of American History" (Cosgrove 1985).

Frederick Jackson Turner told us that America is a strong nation because of the strong individualistic people. He has told us that Americans are a new breed of people forged by the hardships of the forest frontier. Americans are self-reliant, materialistic, and they believe the individual is the prime entity of the nation. In the next few chapters we will see that much of what Frederick Jackson Turner wrote is continuing today throughout America.

Hyperactivity is not only a deeply ingrained feature of American culture by virtue of the special fortitude of those who journeyed to the new land in order to settle it—it was a dire neccessity for survival—but, as a result, it has become linked with other fundamental American values and beliefs. Americans have always believed deeply in material progress. The two words "material" and "progress" are virtually inseparable. Each implies the other in the context of the American experience. (Mitroff and Bennis 1989: 139).

Literature Cited
Barrett, Stephen W. *1979. Indians and fire. Western Wildlands 6(3):17-21.*
Belknap, Jeremy. *1796. The Foresters* I. Thomas & E.T. Andrews Printers, Boston.
Cline, A. C. 1936. The Harvard Forest models. J. For. Vol. 34, No. 12;1046
Clymer, W.B. Shubrick. 1900. *James Fennimore Cooper.* Small, Maynard & Co., Boston.
Compton, Wilson. 1942. National Lumber Manufactures Assn. report. J. Forestry Vol. 40, No. 2: 914
Cosgrove, Denis E. 1985. *Social formation and symbolic landscape* Barnes & Noble, Towata, New Jersey.
DeVoto, B. 1953. *The Journals of Lewis and Clark.* Houghton Mifflin Co.,
Elkins, Stanley and Eric McKitrick. 1954. *A Meaning for Turner's Frontier, Part I: Democracy in the Old Northwest.* Political Science Quarterly, Vol. LXIX (September 1954), pp. 323-339.

Fox, Dixon Ryan (ed.). 1934. *Sources of Culture in the Middle West.*

Gansner, D. A. et. al. 1987. Silvicultural cutting opportunities in oak-hickory forests. Northern Journal of Applied Forestry, Vol. 4, No. 2; 59-63.

Giono, Jean. *The Man Who Planted Trees*

Greeley, William B. 1951.Forests and men. Doubleday & Co., NY

Haynes, Richard W. 1989. An analysis of the timber situation in the United States: 1989−2040. Part II: The future resource situation (draft) USDA Forest Service.

Mitroff, Ian I. and Warren Bennis. 1989. *The Unreality Industry* A Birch Lane Press Book.

McGrath, Robert L. 1989. The tree and the stump. Journal of Forest History, Vol. 33, No. 2; (April 1989); 60-69.

Morrissey, Charles T. 1981. *Vermont.* W.W. Norton & Company.

Perlin, John. 1989. *A Forest Journey—The Role of Wood in the Development of Civilization.* W.W. Norton & Company.

Robbins, Roy M. 1962. *Our Landed Heritage.* University of Nebraska Press.

Taylor, George Rogers. 1971. *The Turner Thesis.* D.C. Heath & Company.

Thorp, Daniel B. 1989. *The Moravian Community in North Carolina* The University of Tennessee Press.

Turner, Frederick Jackson 1920. The frontier in American history. Henry Holt & Co.

LANDSCAPE ART MUSEUMS FOR WORKS MENTIONED

Notch of the White Mountains by Thomas Cole: National Gallery of Art, 4th St. & Constitution Ave. NW, Washington DC 20565

Chapter 2. FORESTRY IN OTHER COUNTRIES OF THE NORTHERN HEMISPHERE

Softwoods dominate forests of the northern hemisphere. The term 'softwood' essentially includes coniferous trees, most of which are evergreen. On the other hand, there are hardwoods most of which are deciduous in that their leaves drop each autumn. There are exceptions to all of the foregoing. Hardwoods dominate forests of the southern hemisphere. By and large softwoods are preferred for construction. They are easier to saw, and nail. Their lighter weight is preferred by construction workers. And probably most important is that by custom people use softwoods for construction.

Hardwoods are preferred for furniture, cabinets, and interior panelling. There are exceptions and hardwoods are sometimes used for construction. Tropical rain forests contain immense volumes of wood. There are many species of tree on a typical parcel of forest. This complicates marketing.

An understanding of American forests requires some understanding of alternatives. International trade of forest products is essential for civic leaders, especially when they are geographically located on the scene of the World's largest flow of wood (United States and Canada).

Russia has so very much timberland, and so very much wood, that our starting point for this discussion is slated. And so very much of the wood in Russia is larch that again, there is the point to start.

If you selected a tree at random in northern New England, there is less than a one percent chance of it being larch. It, like white pine, is a conifer, and a softwood by classification although the wood is denser than most softwoods. However, it is not evergreen because larch trees drop all of their needles in autumn. There are ten species of larch in the northern hemisphere, but only tamarack is native to the northeast and Canada. We also have western larch in Oregon and Washington.

Tamarack grows as far north in Canada as trees are found. However, it is a minor component of the forest. The needles grow in clusters on short spur-like branches. The pale green needles turn golden in autumn and then drop. For a while they appear like straw on the forest floor. The small cones mature in one year and then persist on the tree through winter, after the seed has fallen. It is not a big tree. Our champion is at Jay, Maine. It is 95 feet tall and 3.1 feet in diameter. Foresters measure tree diameter at four and one half feet above ground level and refer to it as diameter breast high (d.b.h.).

Tamarack grows on wet soils, soils that are too wet for other species. Prolonged flooding will kill any tree. Tamarack is one of the few larches that does grow well on wet soils. While we are on that topic, if you do cut the trees that are on wet soil, the soil will become wetter and even turn into a bog. Conversely if you have a wet spot in your pasture you might eventually dry it out by planting trees that are known to drink large quantities of water such as the willows.

Tamarack is intolerant of shade, but it does grow rapidly in its youth. It is seldom used for ornamentals. Larch wood is heavy, strong and durable in contact with the soil but it cracks, splits, is difficult to plane and saw, and fresh cut larch logs don't float (remember this one, it is a major problem in Russia). Furthermore dry larch soaks up water and becomes waterlogged. Larch can be used for low grade telephone poles, low grade railroad cross ties, and fence posts. It is one of our lowest valued species.

Our western larch in Washington, Oregon and British Columbia grows taller than tamarack. Japanese larch grows well in New England. Some species grow well in other regions whereas others do not. Those that readily transplant to other regions usually don't regenerate.

In northern parts of the northern hemisphere there is a band of coniferous trees which encircles the globe. These are spruces, firs, larches, hemlocks, and pines. Deciduous trees (aspen and birch) are mixed in with the conifers. Conifers also grow in other regions.

In international trade, countries prefer to export a finished product rather than raw material such as unprocesssed logs. Since the Korean War (1950-1953) there has been a heavy flow of logs into Japan. The logs are from Maylasia, the Phillipines, and the United States. The flow of logs from nearby Russia has been trivial although recently it has increased to nearly ten percent of Japanese imports. Japan manufactures various products including hardwood panelling for their own construction. Japan is the second largest producer of paper, and paperboard products (following the U.S.). Yes, Japan produces more paper and paperboard than Russia. Very little is exported. It is used internally. The Korean War gave Japan the economic stimulus in this field. They supplied American forces in Korea with construction timbers for hospitals, warehouses etc. It was highly profitable for them. In recent years South Korea has been emulating Japan in producing forest products from imported logs.

There has been a flow of logs from Africa into Rome and Rotterdam for about a century. These are hardwoods and are transhipped throughout Europe. And there is a small flow of logs from the U.S. to Canada.

World flow of lumber and plywood is overwhelmingly dominated by the export of lumber from Canada to the United States. We will delve deeper into the topic when we reach Canada. Some high-valued lumber and plywood are exported from the U.S. to Canada.

World flow of paper and paperboard has been overwhelmingly dominated by export of newsprint and other paper from Canada to the U.S. However, by 1991, in response to recycling in the U.S. along with the economic recession, this trade has plummeted. Canadian shipments of paper to Europe have caused sharply falling pulp (raw material for paper) prices to the detriment of Scandanavian countries.

The geography of Russia is far too complex for this book. Simply stated, the former Russian Soviet Federated Socialist Republics (RSFSR) included Siberia and most of the forested regions of the former USSR. Our discussion is dominantly regards Russia.

Russia has about 50 percent of the timberland in the northern hemisphere, and more than half of the world's softwood timber. Their annual growth of wood per acre is far less than the U.S. or even Scandanavia. The reason is that much of their timberland is old-growth timber. These stands are 200 or more years old and have never been logged. The annual mortality of such stands offsets much of the growth. These old-growth stands are susceptible to fire, insects, and disease.

Most of northeastern Chukchi Aut. Okrug is tundra. Tamyr Peninsula is also mostly tundra. Then there is a band where tree cover is only 2 to 15 percent. South of this is a band where only 30 to 45 percent of the terrain is forested. Rivers flow north which aggravates their use for commerce. The railroads run near the southern border, far removed from main forest areas. There are few roads. Most of Siberia has never been logged. There were not even prison camps in much of the region.

Birch is the dominant hardwood, growing most everywhere. Larch is the dominant softwood. There are seven species of larch which comprise about 38 percent of the total volume. Pine comprises 19 percent, and spruce about 16 percent of the volume. Harvest is dominantly by clearcutting, but only 40 percent of their annual growth is usually harvested. However, there is severe overcutting in the more populated northwest. They do have a great deal of timber, but it is located far from population centers.

Logging operations are labor intensive and inefficient. For example some logging is by electric chain saw. A central electric generator on a sled powers ten or twelve saws. There are stationary cable skidders which are electric powered. About five million Russians plus one million in forced labor camps plus one million unconfined forced laborers have been producing somewhat less than the U.S. has with 1.2 million people. Three hundred and fifty of the more than 1,000 former forced labor camps (in 1985) were felling trees and logging. There were another 35 camps involved in saw milling and other forest-products industries. "Logging has the least developed technology of any forest industry" (Barr & Braden 1988 p. 201).

Problems confronting Russia are exemplified by the forest products industry. There is the low degree of mechanization and automation; underutilization and waste of labor; slack work discipline (except in the prison camps where norms had to be fulfilled before the next meal); low real wages; no reward for performance; shortages of equipment; and low levels of capital investment. The tenets of Communism, which have been drilled into Russians for more than 70 years, include the unacceptability of private ownership of real estate, and the unacceptability of private profit. It will be difficult to reverse these attitudes. The envy of people who do well has been elevated to the highest levels.

Processing of wood through sawmills is frequently done in cities where labor is plentiful. In Barr and Braden's book *The Disappearing Russian Forest* (p.132) they cite Finnish reports that their sawlog imports from Russia (on rails) originate more than 5,000 km distance. "..we would not expect commodities such as saw logs to move thousands of kilometers by rail for conversion and attendant generation of wood waste" (Barr and Braden 1988). In 1974 sixty-four percent of timber and wood products were shipped by rail.

Forced labor camps provided cheap, highly productive, labor. Every worker had a 'norm' to meet prior to the next meal. The objective of forced labor camps was production rather than rehabilitation. Safety was not considered important. There were few hard hats, protective boots, work gloves, and hearing protectors.

General Secretary Andropov (between Breshnev and Gorbachev) was boss of a logging camp in Karelia during World War II. He was responsible for fueling wood-burning locomotives using children as loggers.

Some forest fires are instigated by lightning, but not to the extent in our western states. Some fires have been instigated by discontented incarcerated inebriated hooligans. Russians have led the world in parachuting forest fire fighters into the scene of action (smoke jumpers). They use aerial surveillance to detect most fires.

Christmas tree are much in demand. There are heavy fines for poaching trees. They do have state Christmas tree plantations but production cannot meet the demand. The market waiting line for Christmas trees varies from 2 to 8 hours (Binyon 1983:76).

Russia has been educating more foresters than the remainder of the world combined for many decades. Their are ten forestry schools, some of which have more students than all of U.S. forestry schools combined. For example, in 1989 the U.S. had about 4,500 forestry students, but Petersburg (Leningrad) Institute of Forestry had 12,000 in 1972 with 1,100 professors. As far back as 1929 they had 3,000 students. Moscow Forest Engineering Institute had 10,000 students in 1972. There are also forestry schools at Archangel, Saratov, Tiflis, Vladivostock, Omsk,

HoroTscherask, and Gorigord. The term "university" is applied to a limited number of institutions, no more than one per city. The rest are called institutes. The Ministry of Higher and Medium Special Education has defined curriculums and number of students. There has been only one planned index: the number of students. This number must be fulfilled (Tarnopolsky 1988).

On the next TALK SHOW, where there is a Russian, you might query them if they know of a forester. Generally foresters are well thought of in Russia. Books on Russian life never never seem to include any adverse reference to foresters.

> "During those days (WWII) I saw the marvellously tended Carpathian forests. I spoke with foresters, who told me about the methods they used for taking lumber from the forest without depleting the resource." (Grigorenko, 1980; 271).

Grigorenko, one of the original Bolsheviks and a four-star general, did get free. His memoirs cite the more recent devastation of the Carpathian forests but he doesn't blame the foresters.

Russia has a great many barren lands and treeless sand areas. They have been working to afforest these for many decades. Their are 23,000 tree nurseries. Species planted include Norway spruce and Scotch pine. They have accomplished much reforestation.

After World War II several million German prisoners of war drained swamps and planted trees for seven years before negotiators were able to arrange for the relatively few survivors to be released. The principle negotiator was Alec Cairncross (Cairncross 1983).

Leonid Leonov's novel *The Russian Forest* was available in English in 1970. It is a fascinating tale of two Russian forestry professors from the time of the Tsar until after World War II. It is far more than fiction. It is intertwined with the tale of a great conservation movement that began with the translation of George Perkins Marsh's book *Man and Nature*. More recent books supporting the tale include Douglas Weiner's *Models of Nature* and Mark Popovsky's *The Vavilov Affair* (with Foreword by Andrei Sakharov).

When the Bolsheviks took power in 1917 a modest conservation movement was in effect.

By 1866, Russians were able to familiarize themselves with both Lyell and Marsh, whose seminal works appeared in Russian translation that year. (Weiner 1986)

Thus, Vermont's George Perkins Marsh (who we will focus on in Chapter 5) had far-reaching conservation influence. By the late 1880's the Russian Government was moved to combat the forest and wildlife devastation. After the revolution (1919) Lenin met with a leading Russian conservationist and issued a general decree on conservation. By 1930 there were 70 Zapovednik (wilderness areas). Three of them had more than a million acres. But, then the entire movement was sacked (Weiner 1987). Barr & Braden (p.143) imply there are some still existent although they state the number in existence is hard to estimate and the newer Zapovedniks have included large areas of tundra.

The Vavilov Affair concerns biological genetics, detrimental state interference in science, and most important is the revelation of the KGB method of obtaining evidence from scientists concerning their associates. Political interference in the field of genetics was a setback in agriculture and forestry which will require decades to overcome.

Felix Somary was an Austrian banker at the time of World War I. His memoirs cite his futile efforts to stave off the war with financial leverage. He was an advisor in Washington during World War II. At the end of World War I the Soviets asked him to organize a German consortium to take over the logging of the Tsar's former timberlands. The operation went on for about three years but bureaucratic logging controls, along with problems in world trade of forest products caused him to withdraw from the joint venture (Somary 1984).

The former USSR hard currency earnings were dominated by petroleum ($11.4 billion in 1986), then natural gas ($3.9 billion), and a far distant third place were forest products ($0.175 billion) (Goldman 1978). Earnings from gold bullion and weapons were considerable, but secret.

Russia does have a serious paper shortage and they cannot supply the 3,200 publishing houses with the market demand. Russia produces 1/8th as much pulp per capita as does the U.S. (Barr & Braden 1988; 199)

Those of you in environmental studies won't want to miss reading the 1987 book: *Environmental Policy in the USSR* by Charles E. Ziegler.

CASE HISTORY

Let's go west to Germany and pick up our case history with the German exploitation (meaning logging) of the Russian forests following WWI (Somary 1985). This case history will illustrate that wood can be used as a substitute for most every petroleum product.

GERMANY'S USE OF FOREST PRODUCTS IN A WARTIME ENERGY CRISIS

This is a story which seems unbelievable today. However, this story is very real. I have listed references I am using, at the start, so you may read further into this matter if you so desire.

References for this one case history of Germany and World War II
1. Journal of Forestry 36:495-503. May 38. Utilization of wood under Germany's four-year plan.
2. Journal of Forestry 40:6-11. Jan. 42. Glesinger, Egen. The Impact of War on Forest Industries.
3. Heski, Franz. *German Forestry.* 1938. Yale University Press. (Note page 144 on acquisition of colonies. Did this mean the Ukraine, Poland, Yugoslavia etc. ?)
4. Journal of Forestry 36:821-22. August 38. Review. Johann Albrecht vonMonroy: *Deutschlands Helzwirtschaft.*
5. Comite International deBois Heft 8. June 1936. (Note page 13.)
6. Comite International duBois report. January-March 1936/35.
7. Miller, Douglas. *You Can't Do Business With Hitler.* (Mr. Miller was commercial attache in Berlin for 15 years.)
8. Greeley, William B. 1951. *Forests and Men.* (Pages 154-155.) Doubleday & Company, Inc.
9. Sharpe, Hendee, & Sharpe *Introduction to Forestry* p. 517-520.
10. Shepard and Heske. 1933. European Facts for American Skeptics, J. For. Vol. 31. No. 8; 923-931.
11. Von Monroy. 1934. Development of wood consumption in various countries. J. For. Vol. 32, No. 4;498-499.
12. Shepard, W. 1935. American timberland owners study German private forest practice. J. For. Vol.33, No. 1; 5-27. Note p. 14 'The von Keudell Estate'.
13. Hall, R.C. 1935. The new forest policy in Germany. J. For. Vol. 33, No. 1; 83-84.
14. Heske, Franz. 1935. Correspondence. J. For. Vol. 33, No. 11; 952 NOTE: Heske is essentially quoting from the Frederick Jackson Turner Thesis we discussed in Chapter 1.)
15. Bryant, R. C. 1936. Wood gas as a motor fuel. J. For. Vol.34, No. 8; 816-817.
16. Illick, J. S. Book review, *German Forestry* by Heske. J. For. Vol. 36, No. 6; 617-619.

In 1928 Hermann Goering (Adolph Hitler's Deputy) stated: "I have reached the conclusion that wood could become the raw material for world domination." The occasion was a Nazi party meeting in Munich where there was discussion regarding methods of shifting world power from the Anglo-American Block with their control of oil. Hitler was leading the discussion. A young forester, doing graduate study at the University of Munich, Johann Albrecht vonMonroy, Nazi party member number 27, supported Goering's conclusions with forest economic theory and forest statistics.

What forest products were they considering?
How successful were they in producing these products during the war?
Could these products be used in our continuing energy crisis?
What is the current outlook in the United States?

How did the Germans import so very much wood in the mid-1930's without spending any foreign currency?

How did the Germans build the new-technology manufacturing plants without spending any of their critically short foreign currency?

1928 SCENARIO: There was world prosperity after WWI except for Germany and other central European countries. England had exhausted her wood supplies in WWI and was the world's largest buyer, dominating the trade. The USSR was exporting lumber at very low prices through Felix Somary and his German consortium. German wood imports were trivial. World-wide wood supplies were far greater than demand. Kaiser Wilhelm was chopping wood in Holland. Hitler's 1923 Munich Putsch had failed. The University of Munich had a strong forestry school in the field of forest products. One graduate student, Johann Albricht von Monroy had been active in politics as were many Muncheners.

DIGRESSION

Weinberg, Gerhard L. *World in Balance* pp. 3,5, 96. In Mein Kampf Hitler defined his colonial policy.. which meant the acquisition of territories suitable for German settlement after the disposition of the local population.

Fritz Fischer (Transl by Roger Fletcher) *From Kaiserreich to Third Reich* WWII actually started with Bismark and the Kaiser. The Nazi only continued their *prime* objective of world domination and "Lebensraum" meaning more colonization or expansion for German people.

Gordon Martel, Editor. *The Origins of the Second World War Reconsidered* (The A.J.P. Taylor debate after 25 years.) New information is continually released. For example the original set of Oslo Papers (where the author has never been revealed) is scheduled for release in 1992. Then we will find out if the author was Paul Rosbaud, Editor of Springer Verlag. In the early days of the war an unknown person dropped off a package of papers at the British Embassy in Oslo. The British were dubious of the authenticity, but in later years realized they had a complete set of German scientific developments for the war, including a report on German efforts to develop an atomic bomb, as well as the VI and the VII rockets which later blitzed London.

The one person under Hitler's control who might have put the German atomic program on the right track was the Norwegian Jew Victor M. Goldschmidt, still in occupied Norway. Had

Heisenberg and his colleagues come to a proper appreciation of the man-made element plutonium, Germany might have had an atomic bomb in early 1945 and Hitler might have won the war. (Kramish, Arnold. *The Griffin p. 244).*

Professor Heske's *German Forestry* written in the 1930's while he was at Yale.. page 144.. spoke of the need for Germany to acquire colonies. Heske fully realized he meant "Lebensraum" in the Ukraine, Poland, etc.

Adolph Hitler became Chancellor in 1933 and Goering organized his forest products team of three.

1. Von Monroy to develop and produce the products to replace petroleum.
2. Parchmann (a lumber yard clerk and an early Nazi) was to arrange for the import of large quantities of wood without using any of the critical foreign exchange reserves.
3. Forestry Professor Franz Heske was to handle public relations.

Von Monroy and his new products were discussed in several issues of the Journal of Forestry (Aug 1936 Journal of Forestry. Wood Gas as a Motor Fuel). More important was the report of our Commercial Attache in Berlin, Douglas Miller (May 1938 Journal of Forestry), on new products which included rayon and vistra cloth, wood sugars, and Forsmann wood which was the predecessor of our plastics industry. William Greeley, a former Chief Forester, in *Forests and Men* (pp 154-155) writes of meeting with, but not being fooled by, Von Munroy (von Monroy). However, von Monroy succeeded in his assigned mission. There were the British investors who were conned into investing millions of dollars in a wood sugar plant in Holland. The Germans owned it after their occupation of Holland. There was the case of Fritz Mandel, an Austrian industrialist who had opposed the Nazi at every step. He married Heddy Lamar of Hollywood fame, and a wartime advisor to the U.S. government. Von Monroy conned Mandel into building a large wood gas generating plant in Austria by giving him patents and technical support. German occupation of Austria gave von Monroy his plant at no cost. Mandel escaped to Switzerland.

Most all civilian, and some military vehicles, throughout Europe and Scandanavia were powered by wood gas during the war. Included were large trucks and buses. Expedient modifications of the carburetor and other parts were no problem. Most included a charcoal burner at the rear of the vehicle which created the wood gas.

Parchmann's success is documented by the record on wood imports into Germany. A trivial import of 7,150 cubic meters in 1930 was expanded by 1936 to 2,299,512 cubic meters and no foreign exchange was spent. This should be a classic case of international trade where the German government concealed the centralized operation at their end versus the individual firm negotiations at the other end. Matters were confounded with a set of import permits and other hindrances to free trade. The case history, where Parchmann dealt with Yugoslavian lumbermen, was typical. Initially they were delighted with the sales prospects. They were later compelled to lower their price to attain the needed import permits. Wood was shipped. No money was paid. The deficit grew. The Yugoslavs complained. Parchmann visited them again and convinced them to appoint a joint committee to study the matter. Still no money was paid. But a development exposed Parchmann to all of his suppliers.

The League of Nations had been concerned about the disruption of forest products trade after World War I, and the Russian shipments at cut-throat prices. The League sponsored a Comite International duBois with headquarters in Vienna and headed by Egon Glesinger. He had studied forest products trade at the University of London. Germany was never a member of the Comite. Glesinger's Comite met in Moscow in 1936, and there in the informal discussion by Yugoslavian and other members Parchmann's mode of operation was revealed. They all agreed to hold off shipments until money was paid. This slowed the German wood imports until after they occupied the various nations.

Baron von Keudell tried to disrupt Glesinger's comite at the World Forestry Congress of 1936 at Budapest but he was unable to do so. U.S. Chief Forester, Frank Silcox was at the meeting and quickly recognized the intent of von Keudell who blundered in his opening statement to reveal his true intent.

AFTERWORD:

The Food and Agricultural Organization (FAO) of the United Nations evolved from the Comite International duBois (CIB) of the League of Nations. The Forestry Department of the FAO, headquartered in Rome, publishes statistics concerning supply and demand of forest products; coordinates forestry research; advises member nations on forestry matters; and cooperates with other organizations on forestry matters.

Egon Glesinger worked for the FAO of the United Nations as Director of Timber in Geneva. He retired to Philadelphia in 1969 and Died in 1985.

Von Monroy was not tried at Nurenmberg. He also worked for the FAO. He had a massive heart attack and died at his desk in Rome in 1975.

Franz Heske returned to Forestry School in Germany, eventually became embroiled in other disputes and was released from professorial duties.

Parchmann disappeared in the war although there was a Gestapo leader named Parchmann in Hamburg in the early years of the war.

Professor Kurt Irgolic, at Texas A&M, is indexing all of the papers on the technology developed by the Germans.

Senator Larry Pressler's platform, in his quest for the Republican Presidential nomination of 1980, was going to make America self-reliant from imported petroleum. Included was a wood-gas program.

CHARCOAL is made from wood. Nature through a similar process converted fossilized forests into coal. Wood distillation is the technical name for the process where a steel wagon loaded with hardwood is driven into a large oven, the doors are sealed, and heat is applied without oxygen. The process only requires a few days. It reduces the bulk and weight of wood and makes it more transportable over distance. A ton of charcoal produces twice as much heat (calories) as a ton of wood, but it takes three tons of wood to make the ton of charcoal. Charcoal has excellent heating qualities. Iron, melted down with charcoal fire acquires a high carbon content and thus resist rust. The wrought iron gates and hardware of many European cathedrals have withstood rust for 700 or more years.

GERMAN FORESTRY: About 24 percent of Germany is in forest. Germans are generally considered the originators of highly intensive even-aged forest management. Cutting is by clearing small blocks and then planting a new crop of trees. Every possible space in the forest is used for growing trees. They have a greater number of trees per acre than we would have in the same situation. Every tree is a potential crop tree. Rotations are very long and so the mature trees are large.

Forty-three percent of their wood is Norway spruce; 27 percent is pine and larch; 23 percent is beech, birch, and aspen; and 7 percent is oak. In retrospect their forests are dominated by conifers (softwoods). Pine is planted on sandy soils, and spruce is planted on clay soils. During the wet spring of 1945 we could plan our tank attacks by noting, from a distance (aerial survey), where the pine grew. Sandy soils are easier for tanks to traverse than clay soils.

Forty-four percent of the forest is privately owned by farmers and families; 29 percent is owned by states; 23 percent is by towns and cities; 2.4 percent by corporations; and 1.6 percent by the federal government.

Wildlife is generally owned by the landowner. There are numerous rules and regulations. Foresters are generally government employees.

FRENCH FORESTRY: I just cannot imagine two neighboring nations that are so very different, in most every aspect, as France and Germany. Naturally French forests differ from German. French forests are mostly deciduous with 35 percent of the wood being oak. Their forests are mostly uneven-aged. Sixty-five percent of the forest is privately owned. Forestry training is at Nancy.

French foresters date back to the year 1291 (Bechmann 1990) when appointments to forester were for royalty and other special people. The French people have respected their forests and fought for their collective rights to use forest products. Today's France has about the same amount of forest cover as was the case in the 14th century.

The users regretted the constant reduction, over the centuries, of their collective rights to the forest. It was an important factor in starting the French Revolution (Bechman 1990: 258)

PERCENT OF FOREST PRIVATELY OWNED

Nation	Percent
Norway	81
Sweden	75
United States	74
Finland	70
France	65
Holland	62
Great Britain	61
Brazil	57
Japan	57
Germany	46

Most all of the forest in communist countries is state owned. Canada is also an exception as will be discussed.

SCANDANAVIAN FORESTRY: Norwegian forest owners are dominantly farmers, but in Sweden and Finland the owners are a mix of farmers and other people. Rivers in Sweden flow south which is ideal for floating logs to market. Scandanvian forestry cooperatives have been successful. The dominant timber species throughout Scandanavia are Scotch pine, Norway spruce, aspen, and birch.

Finland leads the world in the mechanization of logging operations. Their multi-function machines fell the trees with hydraulic-powered scissoring action; then tilt the trees to a horizontal position and strip off the branches; then stack the tree-length logs; and all the while a micro-computer head is recording the number and sizes of the felled trees. This latter aspect is valuable information, especially when the operator is being paid a fixed wage plus a production bonus.

Finns have developed various chipping machines and swath harvesters. When wood is chipped in the forest with bark, twigs, and leaves the chips are too dirty to be used for paper and hence this is energy wood, used for hog fuel. Energy wood is lower in value than pulp chips that are to be used for paper. Swath harvesters are used for row thinning of a dense stand. The harvester proceeds into the forest and when it encounters a tree, or trees, it pulverizes them and blows the chips into cubic-meter bags for retrieval by another crew.

CANADA: The British North American Act gave control of forest lands to the various Canadian provinces. The Maritime provinces sold most of theirs to private owners. Quebec and Ontario retained 90 percent of their forest in provincial ownership, and as we proceed west most all forest is in provincial ownership.

Consider the case of Quebec. The northern third is tundra with few if any trees. The central third is Taiga with low non-merchantable scattered trees. The southern third is forest. The northern part of the forest zone is coniferous and the southern part is deciduous (but most is in farmlands). The central part of the forest zone is a mix of coniferous and deciduous.

Provinces generally lease their forests to industry charging a very small stumpage fee (price of standing trees). This enables industry to sell most of their production in the United States thus striving toward the Canadian goal of full employment. When the U.S. complains that this is unfair competition, because of provincial subsidization, the Canadian responding argument is that the standard method of determining stumpage price is the residual value. They are correct, in that the standard way of determining stumpage price is to determine the value of the final product that can be derived from the trees on a specific logging chance; then subtract all of the costs of conversion including transportation to market; then subtract an amount for profit and risk; and the remainder is the stumpage price. Naturally with the cost of transportation from Quebec to Alabama being high the stumpage price is trivial.

Canadians are encountering a major problem in that harvested acreage is not being very well regenerated. For example 2.5 million hectares was logged between 1980 and 1983. Fifteen percent was regenerated successfully by planting; three percent was regenerated by direct seeding; thirty-one percent was regenerated naturally; five percent regenerated into aspen; and the other 46 percent did not regenerate into trees.

SUMMARY: Most of the World's forest, that is in non-communist countries, is owned by individuals, families, and farmers. Forests of the northern hemisphere are more likely to be softwood than hardwoods. Softwoods (conifers) are generally used in construction. Russia has extensive forested areas, but much of this is old-growth timber which has very low growth rates. Larch, a low-valued species, dominates Russian forests. The export of forest products from Russia is trivial compared to their export of petroleum products, natural gas, gold, and armaments.

World-wide international trade of forest products, when measured by volume, is dominated by shipments of lumber and newspaper from Canada to the United States. This is also true if the trade is measured by dollar value, but the United States does import low-valued forest products and exports high-valued forest products. We will find in Chapter 7 that in recent years the dollar value of American forest product exports, to all countries, exceeds the value of our imports.

World-wide, the one country which imports the largest volume of raw logs is Japan. They are large producers of paper as well as lumber and panels (plywood). They use most of their production internally. For several decades prior to 1987 Japan did export large volumes of hardwood plywood to the United States. This plywood was produced from logs imported from Maylasia and other countries. Since 1987 Japan has been importing more plywood panels from the U.S. than they export to the U.S. Japan is a large consumer of lumber and plywood.

Strangely, the USSR exports very little volume of logs or lumber to neighboring Japan. The reasons are more than political. Larch intertwined with Russian lack of forest access are other reasons.

The case history of the use of wood by Germany in World War II illustrates our own potential in the event of a petroleum shortage.

LITERATURE CITED

Barr, Brenton M & Kathleen E. Braden. 1988. *The Disappearing Russian Forest*. Rowman & Littlefield — Hutchinson, London.

Bechman, Roland. 1990. *Trees and Man -the forest in the middle ages* Paragon House, NY

Binyon, Michael. 1983. *Life in Russia*. Pantheon Books, NY

Braden, Kathleen Elizabeth. 1981. *Technology Transfer to The USSR Forest Products Sector*. University of Washington Ph.D. 1981.

Cairncross, Alec. 1980. *The Price of War — British Policy on German Reparations 1941-1949* Basil Blackwell, London (p. 193)

Fischer, Fritz. 1986. (Transl. by Roger Fletcher) *From Kaiserreich to Third Reich*. Allen & Unwin, Boston & Sydney.

Goldman, Marshall I. 1983. Assoc. Director Harvard University Russian Research Center. Personal Correspondence 7/21/83.

Grigorenko, Petro G. 1983 *Memoirs*. WW Norton & Co.

Kramish, Arnold. 1986 *The Griffin*. Houghton Mifflin Company, Boston.

Leonov, Leonid. 1966. *The Russian Forest* — A novel. Progress Publishers, Moscow.

Richards, John F. & Richard P. Tucker. 1988. *World Deforestation in the Twentieth Century* Duke University Press, Durham and London.

Somary, Felix. 1986. Raven of Zurich (p. 140-141) St. Martin's Press, NY.

Tarnopolsky, Yuri. 1988. Soviet Higher Education — A First Hand Report. Academic Questions, Vol. 1, No. 2. Transaction Periodicals Consortium, Rutgers — The State University of New Jersey.

Weiner, Douglas R. 1986. *Models of Nature — Ecology, Conservation, and Cultural Revolution in Soviet Russia* Indiana University Press, Bloomington and Indianapolis.

Ziegler, Charles E. 1987. *Environmental Policy in the USSR.* The University of Massachusetts Press. Amherst.

CHAPTER 3   THE CIVILIAN CONSERVATION CORPS (CCC)

This chapter is about a conservation program that stands far above anything else in the history of conservation the world over. It emanated from the thinking of one person, a President of the United States who referred to himself as a forester. The CCC had the near unanimous support of congressmen, all of our governors, and nearly all editorial writers throughout the United States.

The accomplishments of the program fall into two categories. First the favorable influence on the lives of millions of Americans. The second category were the conservation accomplishments. Certainly work done by the CCC significantly contributed to the situation where we are today. The specter of a timber famine has vanished from the horizon, and we suddenly find that we have an abundance of wood with our annual growth becoming increasingly larger than our annual timber harvest, although wood consumption has risen above all previous records. Even if Canadians were not nice enough to send us two-thirds of the lumber they produce, we would still have an abundance of wood.

There were conservation accomplishments, such as in Vermont's Winooski River Valley, where the liklihood of another 1927 devastating flood, is greatly diminished by the three large Winooski River dams. These were very special CCC projects built by World War I veterans.

This is not solely a history lesson. There are at least ten teaching points which are worth consideration by America's civic leaders. The topic has arisen in most every session of Congress since World War II. The topic regularly arises in state legislatures, county commissioner meetings, and city councils. If your grandfather, or one of your uncles, was in the CCC we are certain that you know about it.

1. Why was the CCC so successful?
2. Why did an organizational structure, which most any authority on organizational behavior would have rejected, work so very well?
3. Each of the thousands of camps had a dual command. What was this duality and was there significant conflict?
4. The nature of the work had little relationship to most enrollee's future careers. So, what was gained?
5. What is gained when legislation is rushed through Congress?
6. Have typical CCC projects depreciated, or appreciated, since the 1930's?
7. How was the Director of the CCC selected?
8. Was President Franklin D. Roosevelt anti-urban? Was he an aristocrat who was incapable of charting a course for urban America (as historian Paul Conklin writes)? Was the CCC merely his method of siphoning off urban discontent by sending young men into the forests?

9. Did F.D.R. attract the nation's finest into Federal Government? Did he support a competitive Civil Service system?
10. The Vermont Professor, John Dewey, was anti-New Deal. "Dewey was never satisfied with the New Deal preferring a more explicitly designed socialism to the vague expediencies." (Sitkoff 1985: 160). Dewey argued that persons most fully realized their individuality in association with others. How did rugged individualists fare in the CCC?

President Roosevelt was a lawyer by training; he had been Assistant Secretary of the Navy in World War I; then he had been crippled by polio, and so badly handicapped that he could scarcely stand without assistance. The American news media of that era were truly great in never showing the President with any infirmity. Hence many people never fully realized the extent of his disability. (This one case would be the best argument for support of our excellent handicapped programs). His positive attitude overcame his handicap and he went on to become Governor of New York State of New York State and then an unprecedented four terms as President. If the American people had fully realized his disability, could he have been elected President four times? (Gallagher 1990).

He never claimed to be a lawyer after being Governor but regularly stated he was a forester. For example, on November 20, 1928, while he was Governor, he wrote "I am also a forester" in a letter to Dean Moon of the New York State College of Forestry (Nixon 1957; Vol. 1;68). The cited reference includes numerous similar statements plus many letters to the Society of American Foresters. He was recognized as a forester by the Society of American Foresters when the lead editorial of the January 1933 issue of the Journal of Forestry was entitled:

Franklin D. Roosevelt — Forester

Earlier he had been elected to associate member in the Society (J. Forestry Vol. 30, No. 3:374. Why did he become a forester? Well for one thing he had experience and a keen interest in tree planting on his Hyde Park estate.   And for another thing, at that time foresters represented the epitomy of public service because the Forest Service had only *one primary objective* which was custodial forest management. Public interest in conservation was widespread due to the Great Crusade, America's first conservation movement. (See Chapter 5).

Not everyone approved of the President's policies but in that era presidents, of any political party, were referred to with their proper title. It was deemed proper that when American people duly elected a person to this honor, he should be respected. Consider another case history: In June of 1847 President Polk, a slave owner, toured the northeast from Philadelphia to Portland Maine. This was the height of the Abolition Movement. He was accompanied by a news reporter, John Appleton. Appleton's diary of Wed July 7, 1847 reads

No President could have ever had a more gratifying Journey. It was crowded with incidents, but not one of them unpleasant. The people bade him welcome, not only to their homes but to their hearts, and were glad to honor themselves, in doing honor to their President..." (Cutler 1986).

President Roosevelt was nominated to be the Democratic candidate for president in July 1932. He had written his own acceptance speech. It included "An immediate means of relief, both for the unemployed and for agriculture will come from converting millions of acres of marginal and unused land into timberland through reforestation...employment can be given to a million men."

We never did attain a million men at one time. At the height of the program there were 520,000 men enrolled. However, in that none could stay for more than one year several million men did serve in the CCC.

There are critics of most any proposal. The CCC was no exception. Some foresters were critical, stating that the first crop of planted trees won't amount to much, and may wither and die, because of the worn out soil. Secretary of Agriculture Hyde (Hoover administration) stated there were not enough available seedling trees to keep a million men busy for three hours. Foresters who were supportive of the plan included James W. Sewall of Old Town, Maine, and Jim Hazard, State Forester of Tennessee.

Inaugeration Day was Saturday March 4, 1933. After the inaugeral service the President drew up his own sketch of the CCC organization. The original, with penmanship that could never have been duplicated by anyone else, has been widely circulated as evidence that this was all the thinking of one President, and not Congress, and not a committee!

The organization plan would have been rejected by most any student of organizational theory. It called for a director to serve directly under the President, along with a small staff (actually about 90 persons). The Department of Labor would enroll qualified youth, the War Department would provide medical examinations, uniforms, equipment, a two-week training period, and transport the enrollees to camps in the forest. There the Department of Agriculture (including the Forest Service) and Department of the Interior (including the Park Service) would take over administration and work.

The President wanted at least 300,000 men working by the first of July. The bill was rushed through Congress in about ten days (originally it was named the emergency relief program and the name CCC was devised later). By mid-April it was apparent the target of 1 July would not be met unless changes were made. Hence the President told the War Department they would have an expanded role which included building the camps and managing the administration for each camp. The Army, under Chief of Staff Douglas MacArthur, responded. Service schools were cancelled and most every available Army officer was diverted into the program. The target date was easily met.

The passage of the legislation by Congress was not without opposition. William Green, President of the American Federation of Labor, felt that it was too much regimentation of labor and the proposed wage rate of one dollar per day would depress all wages. Norman Thomas, of the Socialist Party, felt there would be no lasting effect on unemployment and that it all sounded like the Fascist work camps for youth. The President was not too concerned about the Socialist Party's objections for they had very little political strength. But he was concerned about opposition by organized labor. Being the astute politician that he was he overcame that problem with one stroke. He decided to appoint a labor leader as the program director. He searched his memory and came up with the name of Robert Fechner who had done quite well in solving labor problems back in World War I. The President had known him. Fechner was located at Harvard University where he was teaching labor relations. He had come a long way from his starting career in the machine shop of the Georgia Railroad at age 14. In retrospect the President could not have made a better selection. He also selected a labor leader, James J. McEntee, as Assistant Director.

In early June of 1943 the President invited William Green (AF of L) to accompany him on a visit to Camp Roosevelt, a CCC camp in western Virginia. At the end of the day William Green told the President that he believed that this was going to be a truly great program. He apologized for his initial opposition. (Note the President's mode of operation. This will be developed further in Chapter 5.)

The President stated there were two objectives: conservation work and unemployment relief. The New York Times, March 31, 1933 wrote: "There will be employment for hundreds of thousands along with regaining our lost forest lands." The New York Herald Tribune (opposed to the President) wrote: "Will the program ever justify the expenditure? But the CCC promises well to reduce unemployment." This latter statement, by an opposition newspaper, seemed to set a neutral trend that pervaded the opposition newspapers throughout the nation for the next nine years regards the CCC.

Not only was President Roosevelt to shape the CCC into a great program, but the CCC was the program which transformed the President from a politician to a great leader.

> One of the first stages in the development of the hero is The Call to Adventure, i.e., the happenstance, event or circumstance that elevates the aspiring hero from his/her everyday life—or ordinary reality—into a new, totally unexpected reality that will

test and develop the person, if he/she is successful in meeting certain challenges, into a genuine hero....This is why the best heroes are shaped as much by external circumstances not fully under their control as they are by formal training and education. (Mitroff and Bennis 1989: 150).

THE INFLUENCE OF THE PHYSICALLY CHALLENGING WORK ON THE YOUTH

There is considerable evidence that physically challenging forestry work effects a marked improvement on the immediate, and life-long behavior of participants. The effect is even carried through to descendants and associates. We saw this general concept in Chapter 1, but it is so important to us that a few thoughts will be repeated.

Frederick Jackson Turner's 1893 Thesis is recognized as the most influential single piece of historical writing ever written in the United States (Taylor 1971). Turner concluded that rigors of coping with forest frontiers had forged the American, who was far more individualistic, self-reliant, inventive in nature, and powerful to effect great ends than had been his European ancestors. Thus our forest frontier individualism had promoted democracy. Our frontier line ceased to exist about 1890 but the individualism, and recognition of individual worth, that our forest frontiers imparted to our forefathers has been passed on to present generations. There has also been a furtherance of American individualism through our unequaled opportunities of owning agricultural and forest lands. This partnership, between forests and Americans, has been instrumental to our continued freedom.

The Civilian Conservation Corps (CCC) of the 1930's "shouldered through a volume of work that stands above anything in the annals of conservation the world over" (Greeley 1951). William Greeley was Chief Forester of the United States and had also commanded the Forest Engineer Regiment of the American Expeditionary Force in France during World War I. However, even the stupendous work accomplishments mentioned by Greeley are miniscule in comparison to the effect of the forest work on behavioral attitudes of three million Americans, their families, descendants, and associates. Judge J. M. Broade, of the Chicago Boy's Court, stated "The CCC is largely responsible for the 50% reduction in the Chicago crime record during the last four years" (New York Times, October 2, 1936, p. 6). The New York City Commissioner of Corrections attributed large decreases in youth crime to the CCC (New York Times, February 17, 1937, p. 1 and 10 of the General News Section).

The CCC did make youth more employable. During the 6-month enrollment period ending 3/31/34, 3,726 men were discharged from the

CCC to accept outside employment (American Forests, July 1934). It is important to our deliberations today that we recognize these jobs had little relationship to the CCC work. The CCC men developed a good work ethic and this is what carried them through into gainful employment. Some CCC camps maintained a "Top Ten Best Worker List" (camps generally had 200 enrollees) and prospective employers interviewed therefrom. The CCC men vied to be on the list. Employers hired from these lists. The Burlington (Vermont) Free Press of December 15, 1936 reported 12,000 young men leaving the CCC monthly for other employment.

The CCC men were afforded the opportunity of demonstrating the prowess they had developed in state-wide woodsmen contests (Burlington Free Press, July 12, 1934, p. 2).

A comparison of CCC death rates, per 100,000 population, against the national average showed the CCC had 1.0 by alcoholism against 3.3 nationally; homicides were 1.6 in the CCC against 9.3 nationally; and suicides were 0.8 in the CCC against a national 16.8 (American Forests, November 1934). There is at least one story which indicates alcoholism was not widespread in the CCC. "Enrollee in CCC camp ordered out of state...Fred C... of Brookline, Massachusetts was ordered out of state after pleading guilty to a charge of intoxication" (Burlington Free Press, June 13, 1936).

The CCC was not an extension of high school. Some men did learn skills that were useful to them throughout the remainder of their lives, but the most general achievement was the development of a work ethic. Perry H. Merrill, State Forester of Vermont during the CCC era and still active in civic, forestry, political, and literary matters in 1991, writes, "They learned to be punctual, to take orders from their superiors, to accept responsibility, to be disciplined and learned to cooperate with others" (Merrill 1981). The Director of the CCC, Robert Fechner, wrote, "We do everything we can to fit enrollees for a useful life, but the CCC is a work centered organization and not a substitute for high schools and colleges. It is, however, a practical school where young men in their teens and early twenties are taught how to work, how to live and how to get ahead" (Fechner 1939). James McEntee was Assistant Director of the Corps and took over as Director when Fechner died. He wrote, "As men, they will be better workers, better neighbors and better citizens. Already more than two million of them have had their baptism of real work and training in the CCC. Now they are men!" (McEntee 1941). Glen Kovar wrote, "It was a case of *men building forests and forests building men*. It was one of the finest hours..." (American Forests, May 1936).

There was at that time, as there is today, a tremendous work backlog on our public forests. CCC men knew they were accomplishing useful work and this was far more relevant to them than learning some specific skill. Robert Fechner, Director of the CCC, in a letter to President Roosevelt, dated April 14, 1939, included, "I believe the general popularity of the Corps is due in large measure to the belief of the general public that it has not been conducted as a welfare organization but has engaged in useful worthwhile work that has added substantially to the wealth of the Nation" (Nixon 1957). L. S. Taber was an educational advisor to the CCC. His talks and lectures were often reprinted and distributed to camp libraries. His writings include, "we must dignify and glorify work with the hands, lifting vocational activity to the dignity of professional service... we must lift manual toil, successfully and well performed, to the nobility and dignity of the highest place in the life of the race. This alone will answer the need of the hour. The enrollee must see that he is an important cog in the world's machinery and that he must learn to take his place and do his work" (Lacy 1976).

In 1934, Major General Johnson Haywood wrote, "Perhaps the Country would be better off if some of our big businessmen, bankers, and politicians had been to CCC camps in youth" (American Forests, July 1934). This is where we are today and we are better off for it. There are leading citizens across the nation who would never have risen to these responsibilities had they not been in the CCC. Congressman Dan Daniels (Virginia, eighth term) wrote, "I was enrolled in this program (CCC) for two years. We contributed to our national wealth by building parks, roads and power projects" (Daniels 1982). In 1976, Howell published the stories of nearly 150 CCC alumni as seen from their later years. Most of their life work had little relation to their CCC duties, but their stories attribute the success they attained to their CCC work ethic. Most of the work was of a forestry nature. There are alumni who did learn specific occupations for their future careers. "Keith (Arasmith) learned to operate heavy equipment, an occupation that has stayed with him most of his life. Knowing how to operate the equipment really helped him during World War II as he joined the 802nd Aviation Engineers and was in charge of heavy equipment on Atka Island in the Aleutian Chain" (Howell 1976).

In the 1960's, John Salmond, a New Zealander, was studying history at Duke University. His advisor inspired his interest in the CCC. There resulted a scholarly study of the CCC from a very impartial source. "Finally, the CCC had a lasting effect on its enrollees. Life in the camps brought tangible benefits to the health, educational level, and employment expectancies of almost three million young Americans, and it also gave immediate financial aid to their families. Equally important were the intangibles of Corps life. The CCC gave its enrollees both an understanding of their country and a faith in the future" (Salmond 1967).

President Roosevelt repeatedly affirmed the two objectives of the CCC as being the accomplishment of conservation work and the relief of unemployment. Both he and Fechner resisted every attempt to broaden the objective of the program, particularly by those who would have used the Corps as an instrument to inflict their political, social and economic ideas on our youth. One example would be the skirmish between the American Association of University Professors (AAUP) and Fechner. (New York Times, Nov. 16 and 25, and Dec. 2, 1934). The AAUP resolution read

"What the boys in the CCC need is a broader education that will give them a true picture of the current industrial and social problems" J. W. Crabtree, Secretary.

The success of the CCC is largely attributed to the strength of the Director in adhering to the conservation work objective. The other objective (relieving unemployment) was redundant because of widespread unemployment at that time. *There really was only one objective.* "As soon as governmental activity has more than one purpose it degenerates." (Drucker 1989). President Roosevelt and Fechner realized there would be other values. In President Roosevelt's letter to Congress (March 21, 1933) he proposed a civilian conservation corps and emphasized the value of the forest work that would be accomplished. He went on to say, "More important, however, than the material gains will be the moral and spiritual value of such work" (Nixon 1957)

Initially, the opposition was from organized labor and the Socialist Party as we have earlier discussed. During the life of the CCC there were a few individuals who did not feel the CCC was successful. The dissension was based on two points. First, physical accomplishments would not have compared with skilled woodsmen, and it would have been better, economically, to have only employed proficient woodsmen. The only clear documentation of CCC work accomplishments per man-hour of time was compiled by Austin Hawes, State Forester of Connecticut. His compilations (Hawes 1936) indicate the accomplishments per man hour left much to be desired. But there is far more to life than economic quantifications.

Secondly, there were also those who felt the CCC tended to build too many roads which were detrimental to wilderness values. However, as Hawes explains, forest work requires access roads (Hawes 1936). Be this as it may, the nation's editors were in accord regards the success of the CCC as determined by a study of the editorials during the late 1930's when the CCC was being considered as a permanent organization (Salmond 1967). The 1936 "Congressional Revolt" was Congress's refusal to trim the size of the CCC, which the President had requested in order to balance the budget. In the ensuing presidential political campaigns, President Roosevelt's opponents endorsed continuation of the CCC. It was discontinued in 1942 because of manpower needs of World War II.

The influence of physically challenging forestry work on CCC men was vital to our victory in World War II. The Director of the CCC foresaw the situation. "Many of the young men now in camps will enter the nation's armed forces. When that time comes, they will be better prepared to serve their country because of the discipline, the training, and the physical hardihood they have gained in the Civilian Conservation Corps" (McEntee 1942). Even though military training such as rifle marksmanship and parade drill were not a part of the CCC, they did wear uniforms and otherwise lived in a military manner. In the late 1930's, when the war clouds were darkening, there was pressure to include rifle marksmanship military training in the CCC, but again Fechner said no.

THE ENROLLEES

Enrollees had to be unmarried young men between the ages of 17 and 23, not attending school, preferably with families to whom they could allot $25 monthly. They had to be citizens of the U.S.A. There were additional criteria established which just could not be enforced: good moral character, not on probation, physically qualified, willing to stay for at least six months, and never convicted of an offense carrying a prison sentence of more than one year.

Most enrollees were city youth and 77 percent were 19 years of age or under. The drop-out rate was very high, with approximately 12 percent deserting camp, many after only three or four days. Discharges for disciplinary reasons were eight percent. Applicants far exceeded slots but admission selection brought in youth who just were not prepared to mix in with 200 young men from different parts of the country. Many of these were rural youth, who with different management might have performed very well. Some were in the "potential leader" category referred to by Mitroff and Benis (1989) "Right now, there are probably several hundred thousand potential leaders in America — young passionate men and women full of promise with no outlets for their passion, because we scorn passion even as we reward ambition. If we can trust history, they're more likely to be the loners, the kids who always seem to be a bit at odds with their peers, off there, looking at life from an odd angle. Leaders are always originals, not copies."

World War I veterans conducted their second bonus march on Washington in 1933, and stated they would not leave until they were paid the bonus they had been promised for the 1940's. the President had his wife, Eleanor, and Harry Hopkins discuss alternatives with the veterans. This was in sharp contrast with the first bonus march which occured when

President Hoover was in office where the veterans were chased out of town by the Army under command of General MacArthur. Eleanor Roosevelt reached a solution and the veterans left Washington. The solution was that the veterans, now in their forties, would be admitted to the CCC in special units and paid the full $30 per month. They were not to be mixed in with the younger youth. About 25,000 so enrolled and many were assigned to build the three Winooski River dams in Vermont under the supervision of the Corps of Engineers. Each of the three camps had about 2,000 veterans which was ten times larger than regular camps.

Native Americans wanted to be in the program and yet live at home on the reservation. Projects were established on reservations for 14,400. Eleven percent of the enrollees were African Americans and generally served in separate units. There were numerous exceptions as shown on our cover. In 1935 forty-seven camps were established for young women. This program was more educational than conservation work.

By and large, enrollees had a superb attitude. Holland & Hill (1942) conducted studies one of which included 7,000 enrollees. They found that 63 percent had enrolled to help their families with the $25 monthly allotment; 91 percent stated their family understands and helps them; 77 percent agreed their school courses had been very good; 65 percent agreed that they became more interested in the job itself than in the earnings; 75 percent felt the CCC experience would get them to like hard work; and 61 percent agreed the best benefit would be their better chances of getting a job when they left the CCC. Please note this was an era when $25 would pay the monthly rent for a large four or five bedroom city home.

These financially deprived children of the Great Depression did not blame others for their financial woes, nor did they envy the wealthier class. They had not been incited to vandalize property of the wealthy by aspiring politicians. They did have ambition and they knew they were going to succeed in life. This was the generation "which had a rendevous with destiny" quoting President Roosevelt in his speech at Franklin Field in Philadelphia in July 1936*. This was the G.I. Generation in *Generations* by William Strauss and Neil Howe, 1991.

---

*Few people ever realized that, upon entering Franklin Field and leaving his limousine, the President's leg brace had become unlocked, he had fallen to the ground. The pages, with his written speech had been scattered over the field. Part extemporaneously, the President delivered his most confrontational speech, alienating big business. It brought an ovation that has seldom been equaled.

THE ADMINISTRATORS

The Director had a 92-person staff. Secretary of Labor, Frances Perkins, superbly administered enrollment. General Douglas MacArthur, along with most every available Army officer, was directly or indirectly involved in the CCC. About one-third of the regular Army officers were assigned to one of the camps intially. Eventually some were replaced with reserve officers. Generally, there were four officers per camp, one of whom was a physician. This was the era of measles, polio, whooping cough, tuberculosis, and other diseases which aggravated the many underweight, undernourished, newly enrolled young men. A physician was needed at each camp. Many had never seen a dentist.

Secretary of Agriculture Henry Wallace, later Vice President, was superbly qualified for his association with the CCC. Secretary of the Interior, Harold Ickes, although highly controversial at times, was a staunch supporter of the President and his CCC. The President had brought the best qualified people to Washington and not his former cronies. No student of organization would have recommended a plan that encompassed these four cabinet-level organizations working together, since prior to this (and also afterwards) there was usually a discordant tone. However, the system worked beautifully because of the high quality of the cabinet officers and General MacArthur.

Each camp also had local experienced men (L.E.M.'s) as crew leaders. These jobs were eagerly sought because they paid well. State-level politics did enter the hiring in some cases. However, the Society of American Foresters, under the leadership of Professor Hermann H. Chapman of Yale School of Forestry, were able to destroy the spoils system in the public administration of the CCC. See the April and May 1934 issues of the Journal of Forestry for details. Some writers have attributed political bias in the acceptance of enrollees, but this is not correct. The voting age (and political registration in certain states) was 21 at the time. Few of the enrollees were old enough to vote. Furthermore, Mrs. Perkins would never have tolerated such practice.

After 1935 camps had an education director who offered evening courses in high school subjects. Few youth desired such instruction after a hard day's work. Some camps required a specific level of attendance, but then enrollees slept in class. The preferred evening entertainment was boxing with 16 ounce gloves.

THE CONSERVATION WORK

Many camps were on state forests and parks because most of the youth were in the east where the various states did own forests. On the other hand, most national forests were in the west.

Table 2. MARCH 1934 STATUS OF THE MAIN CCC CAMPS

Location	Number of Camps
State forests and parks	571
National forests	432
Private lands	337
	(These will be discussed)
National parks	61
Other federal	13
TVA (Tennessee Valley Adm.)	25
	1,439

Accomplishments on federal lands alone included more than 1.5 billion trees planted, many of which are now sawtimber sized and contributing to our well being. More than three million acres underwent timber stand improvement whereby the trees which had no potential for sawtimber were removed to better utilize the forest space. These acres have far greater annual growth today than they would otherwise have had. More than 17 million acres were treated for tree diseases and insects. This acreage is far more productive as a result. There were nearly eight million firefighting man days. The nation's fire losses dropped to 17 percent of what they had been just before the CCC era, but just as important was the ushering out of the age when local citizenry were the third-line of forest fire defense. (Note: in the early days of the depression many job fires were instigated by persons who expected to be hired to suppress the same fire. The mobilization of the CCC nullified this source of employment. Hence job fires generally stopped. This was the main reason for the amazing drop in fire losses.

More than four million small dams were constructed to check erosion on farms. There were 98,000 miles of truck trail constructed, most of which are critical to the forest management today. A few of these roads are now main ski trails. Also included were 45,350 buildings, and 41,303 bridges many of which are so constructed, of stone masonry, that they may well survive until the next glacier.

The 3,489 fire lookout towers, and the 66,161 miles of telephone line thereto, on federal lands did serve their purpose. However, they have generally been replaced by aerial detection along with even newer detection methods. There were similar accomplishments on state lands.

Instruction in building trades was never a stated objective. If it had been organized labor might not have been very supportive. Thousands of plumbers, electricians, carpenters, and stone masons were trained. In 1975 a former CCC inspector, Jim Caylor, told our associate that the President and Fechner had never publicized this aspect of the CCC for fear of alienating organized labor. (Caylor, 1973)

THE SHELTERBELT, OR PRAIRIE STATES FORESTRY PROJECT

Black Sunday is a memory etched forever into the minds of most Americans who were living on April 14, 1935. The sun was blotted from the sky, throughout the prairie states, by dirt blowing from rangeland which should never have been plowed. The towering dirt clouds were visible as far distant as Philadelphia. This was not the first, nor the last, dust storm. But, one forester, travelling by train through Montana, had the idea that huge belts of trees could ameliorate the situation. The forester was President Franklin D. Roosevelt. No, the shelter belt project did not emanate from a committee, nor from Congress, nor from research. It came from one mind.

There was immediate opposition from those who felt trees would never survive. Fortunately, there had been advance work done and the state forester of North Dakota, the extension forester of Wyoming, and the Dean of the College of Agriculture in Nebraska were supportive.

Many early plantings were by the CCC, but later other agencies were included. Plantings included 223 million trees, stretching 18,600 miles across 30,000 farms and ranches, in mile-long 8 to 10 row segments, forming a discontinuous band 100 miles wide. Shelter belts have been conserving our soils, along with providing ideal wildlife habitat and numerous other amenity values, for more than fifty years. An excellent reference is R. Douglas Hurt. *The Dust Bowl.*

CIVILIAN CONSERVATION CORPS PROJECTS ON PRIVATE LAND

In August 1937 Robert Fechner, Director of the CCC, wrote President Roosevelt that there were 528 CCC camps operating on privately owned land. However, the limitations on the nature of the work and the President's personal supervision resulted in few if any criticisms for using public funds on private lands. Today this situation is difficult to comprehend. But, the comprehension is vital when one considers the importance of privately owned forest lands in supplying our needs.

Franklin D. Roosevelt was the first recipient of The Society of American Forester's Sir William Schlich memorial medal (1935). He had a good understanding of the small forest land owners. In 1931 he wrote: "The owners are nonresidents or old people in most cases. We cannot expect them to do any reforestation."(Nixon 1957).

When President Roosevelt broached the idea of the CCC at the Democratic Convention in 1932 James O. Hazard, Tennessee State

Forester, came to the defense of the CCC concept. He sent a copy of his paper to the President who immediately acknowledged the letter with thanks. Hazard's paper included:

> It is my opinion that there are vast areas in all of the Southern States on which the landowners would welcome tree planting, provided it were done at Government expense. I also believe that these landowners would be willing to enter some reasonable agreement to permit the Government to reimburse itself from the sale of timber resulting from such plantings, when such timber became suitable for market. I understand that such a plan provided the means for the reforestation of the Landes in France.

The ACT FOR THE RELIEF OF UNEMPLOYMENT, approved March 31, 1933, which enabled President Roosevelt to establish the CCC, included the following in accord with a specific request of the President.

> That the President may in his discretion extend the provisions of this Act to lands owned by counties, and municipalities and lands in private ownership, but only for the purpose of doing thereon such kinds of cooperative work as are now provided for by Acts of Congress in preventing and controlling forest fires and the attacks of forest tree pests and diseases and such work as is necessary in the public interest to control floods (Nixon 1957)

The Tennessee Congressional Delegation urged the use of Federal funds to correct erosion problems in western Tennessee. In his May 1933 reply President Roosevelt stated:

> the Federal government cannot properly undertake to reforest privately owned lands without some provision for getting its money back when the timber matures. If the State of Tennessee could make some arrangement to attain this end with the owners of the land, that would be a different story. I know you will see the objective. As a matter of fact, there is plenty of Federal and State owned land to keep us busy for a year or two. In the meanwhile it is worth exploring the private land problem (Nixon 1957).

President Roosevelt wrote Robert Fechner, Director of the CCC in 1937:

> While it is legal to undertake projects on land belonging in private ownership, I think it is a great mistake to do any more of this than we can possibly help. There are cases where the cutting of firebreaks, for example, on privately owned forest lands, will safeguard public lands against fire. It is difficult to say to one private owner "We will work on your land" and to his neighbor say "We will not work on your land." (Nixon 1957).

In response, Fechner wrote a detailed letter to the President outlining the nature of work that was being done on private lands. (The President responded three days later stating that the program outlined had his full approval.)

Fechner described three phases of work being done on private lands. First were 113 CCC camps on forest protection where all work was being done to carry out state or community protection plans. Secondly was work being done in the reconstruction of drainage systems by 41 CCC camps. And 374 CCC camps were engaged in erosion protection work.

There were political pressures on the Director of the CCC, but being a Presidential appointee, a man of strong conviction, and being in full accord with the President, enabled Fechner to hold the line. In November 1937 one Senator exerted pressure on Fechner to have the CCC camps build new irrigation ditches on a privately owned irrigation district. The President was queried and responded:

> The answer is "no". Do not extend these irrigation projects on private lands except in very rare cases in dry areas where the farmers are practically on relief.

Henry Wallace, Secretary of Agriculture, forwarded a Forest Service proposal to the President in March 1938 that had far reaching implications. This proposal involved two problems: the need to use private forest lands for CCC work because the backlog of work on public lands was rapidly being exhausted; and the need to increase wood production on cutover lands held in private ownership. There was included a bill to facilitate the action.

Ensuing, was a special message to the Congress from the President; a Joint Congressional Committee; hearings held in various parts of the country; the presentation of hypothetical cases to the President; the designation of the plan as the National Cooperative Reforestation Plan; helpful suggestions from the President to the effect that there was a difference between "wood-lot forestry" and "commercial forestry" and that the President saw no need for subsidizing lumber companies; revisions to the plan; studies of the French "Audiffred Law"; the introduction of H. R. 969 in early 1941; and a note from President Roosevelt to the Director of the Bureau of the Budget stating:

> In regard to H. R. 969, there is no such thing as a mixture of woodlot management and commercial forestry. If you want further instruction on growing trees, come and talk with me!
> F.D.R.

The war voided the problem of providing addiitional work for the CCC. The CCC and National Cooperative Reforestation Plan became history.

THE RATE OF WORK

Conservation programs, employing mostly city youth, just cannot be expected to match the accomplishments of skilled woodsmen. The only documented report on the rate of CCC work was by Austin Hawes. It is evidence that the highly regarded CCC placed greater emphasis on quality of work than rate of work. This is only natural when you have so very much available labor. For example tree planting was well done with exceptionally good survival. However, 4.4 man days per acre, after the site had been prepared, is four times greater than would be expected.

Excerpts from Journal of Forestry — July 1936
THE C.C.C. AS AN AGENCY FOR STAND IMPROVEMENT
By Austin F. Hawes, State Forester of Connecticut
(and formerly State Forester of Vermont)

In view of the great good which has been accomplished in many forest regions by the C.C.C., it seems very unfortunate that so much criticism should be leveled at it by foresters.

Factors which have made for inefficiency have been the shortness of the working hours; the fact that camps have never been kept up to authorized strength; the large overhead used by the Army, often without adequate supervision; the lowered age limit for enrollees, which has brought into the camps a lot of boys of underweight and understrength; and the impossibility of keeping first-class men indefinitely. Much money was wasted in enlarging the C.C.C. and building new camps to be used only for a brief period. The educational setup has cost more than results warranted. Most of the real instruction is still given by foremen. In spite of these and other weaknesses, the C.C.C. is a wonderful agency if properly used. Some foresters not connected with the organization have been inclined to criticise the relatively small amount of timber stand improvement accomplished. However, a good road system is fundamental to the practice of forestry. Wherever forests have been developed with truck trails, this work should be considered fully as important as stand improvement. Since my own experience with the C.C.C. has been mostly in Connecticut, this article will deal with our work here. Table 1 shows the distribution of labor by major projects from the time the first Connecticut camps were established up to January 31, 1936.

Table 1. Distribution of Man-Days in Connecticut C.C.C. Camps, by Projects

Project	Number of Man-Days	Percent
Truck and foot trails	480,630	33.1
Forest stand improvement	304,089	21.0
Insect and disease control	240,223	16.6
Fire prevention and control	122,482	8.4
Recreational developments	119,457	8.2
Maintenance(1)	90,444	6.2
Surveys and type maps	68,844	4.7
Administrative structures	20,153	1.4
Miscellaneous	4,436	.3
Total:	1,450,758	100.0

(1) Includes maintenance of trails, structures, picnic areas, fire towers.

In deference to the agitation for wilderness areas, one of our wildest and most picturesque blocks of 1,800 acres has been left entirely undeveloped with truck trails. Up to date 105 miles of truck trail have been completed. Omitting the wilderness area mentioned above, this is an average of one mile of road to every 611 acres.

One of the outstanding accomplishments of the Connecticut C.C.C. has been converting the State Highway Department away from concrete to creosoted hardwood fence posts. Preliminary experiments had convinced the Department that hardwoods were practicable, but it would not incorporate these in their specifications unless assured of a definite supply. The C.C.C. set up a small creosoting plant and cut and treated 27,050 posts of oak, soft maple, birch, and beech. This project utilized 5,196 man-days in creosoting, and 2,247 mandays in transporting the posts to the plant. Now that it has proved a success, the plant has been leased to a fence contractor and Connecticut farmers are assured a market for their thinnings which they would not have had except for this initial C.C.C. work.

Planting: An average of 15.8 man-days per acre for planting is due to the fact that the Forest Service requires that "preparation of land for planting" be charged under this heading instead of to "reproduction cutting," where it properly belongs. As most of the open land in Connecticut state forests has already been planted, the C.C.C. men have been employed in cutting off stands of gray birch, alder, and other worthless growth and planting it. Since the brush is piled and burned, the preparation requires about 22 man-days per acre while the actual planting requires about four man-days.

Treatment of Natural Stands. — The weeding in young hardwoods requires four man-days per acre, just as in plantations. The purpose is to free enough hardwoods of valuable species to make a stand.

Of course there are various reasons why some of the other states have not done much in stand improvement. Many states either do not have state forests or the forests are so poor that they offer little opportunity for work other than planting. In Massachusetts the interests of the Conservation Commissioner were wholly in recreational developments. Probably the success or failure of the C.C.C. in stand improvement work depends largely upon the selection of the supervisory personnel. In states having a large proportion of politically appointed foremen it is probably better that little stand improvement has been undertaken.

Table 5 ANALYSIS OF COST PER CORD IN C.C.C. MAN-DAYS OF STAND IMPROVEMENT

Operation	Cords produced	Cords per acre	Chopping/ sawing, man-days per cord	Brush disposal, man-days per cord	Removal of products, man-days per cord	Tot
Improvement cutting	5,411,5	4.2	3.7	.2	1.0	4.9
Weeding young stands	206.7	.3	6.4	--	--	6.4
Preparation for planting	1,347.0	4.0	3.8	3.9 .5	8.2	
Total	7,062.5	3.2	3.8	.9	.9	5.6
Overhead, man-days			.6	.1	.2	.9
Total, including overhead			4.4	1.0	1.1	6.5

Robert Fechner died in office shortly after American Forests had published his paper "My Hopes for the CCC" in the January 1939 issue of American Forests. The paper included the annual cost per enrollee had been about $1,000 in 1938. Total costs to date were 2 billion dollars (23 percent of which was sent to the families). The CCC is a work-centered organization, not a substitute for high school. It is, however, a practical school (Fechner 1939).

The CCC was deactivated in 1942 because of the manpower needs of the War. The leaders, at that time, realized that eventually there would be other such programs, so they wrote out their recommendations for future civic leaders. Conrad Wirth was Director of the National Park Service and also Department of the Interior's representative on the CCC Advisory Council. His final report in 1943 included.

1. There is a continuing need for conservation programs.
2. The CCC made the country aware of conservation needs.

3. The CCC strengthened our human resources.
4. There should only be one main objective, and never the relief of unemployment.
5. One-year service limitation emphasized preparation for a better job.
6. The success depended on the ability of the Director.
7. The trend to build up a school-room type of educational program and impractical (and unpopular courses) in the camps caused a conflict of understanding the real objectives.

SUMMARY

The CCC was a very successful federal programs. This is evidenced by the results and by the dearth of critics. It was a quintessential conservation program which may never again be attained. The higher-level administrators were such great people that, an otherwise flawed organizational structure, functioned superbly well. The dual command of the camps, despite a few personality conflicts, permitted the Army to concentrate on administration whereas foresters were free to concentrate on conservation work. Enrollees learned the essentials for a successful career rather than a specific skill or trade which might have become obsolete. The rapid Congressional passage of enabling legislation precluded lobbying organizations diluting the objective.

The excessive drop-out rate was primarily due to mishandling of the "loner". These rugged individualists could have been the finest of the enrollees. This was evidenced during the ensuing war where in the direst hour of need young loners, like Audie Murphy, went on to heroism where their sacrifices for the good of their outfits has seldom been paralleled. But, primarily this case history is a vivid illustration of what one civic leader, who had great ideas, can do when they have the self confidence to proceed without referring ideas to committees. President Roosevelt drafted the organization; he selected the director; his cabinet officers were selected on merit and not cronyism; and he sent young city youth to work in the woods since he knew the favorable effect it would have on the youth and on America. This case history has also demonstrated the President's cooperative, non-confrontational style of dealing with problems. His assessment of the non-industrial private forest owners was right on mark!

There were other factors which may well have contributed to the success of the CCC. Recent research has revealed the probability that pine trees have a subliminal scent (below the sense of awareness) which favorably affects human behavior. And in their book Generations William Strauss and Neil Howe develop President Franklin Roosevelt's 1936 observation

> "There is a mysterious cycle in human events. To some generations much is given. Of other generations much is expected. This generation has a rendezvous with destiny." (FDR 1936, Franklin Field, Philadelphia)

Strauss and Howe contend that four types of generations, each with its own salient character traits, have recurred throughout American History. The G.I. generation (born 1901-1924) were of the "civic" type; Heroic rebuilders of the public world, rational and selfless, but capable of being insensitive. Thomas Jefferson is cited as a typical member of a previous "civic" generation. And the Millenial generation born in 1982 or later are our latest "Civic" generation. Strauss and Neil emphasize the cooperative team-work approach of the G.I. generation. Strauss and Howe scarcely mention the CCC, but the CCC fits beautifully into their theory.

The reader can readily connect his community with the CCC, and the shelterbelt project, through the micro-films of the 1930's newspapers in most any library.

LITERATURE CITED

Armstrong, F.H. 1971. Civilian Conservation Corps revival. J. Forestry 69:224-225.

Armstrong, F.H. 1975. Civilian Conservation Corps revival. J. Forestry 73:358-359.

Armstrong, F.H. and Kelley, R.G. 1976. Reactivating the Civilian Conservation Corps. J. Forestry 74:639.

Armstrong, F.H. 1977. Youth programs in conservation. J. Forestry 75:786-788.

Armstrong, F.H. 1977. Civilian Conservation Corps projects on private land. The Consultant 22(3):67-69.

Armstrong, F.H. 1977. Jobs for youth. American Forests 83(11):30-33, 42-44.

Armstrong, F.H. 1979. Report of the task force on CCC legislation. J. Forestry 77:450.

Caylor, James 1973. Audio-tape interview.

Cutler, Wayne. (ed). 1986. *North for Union—John Appleton's Diary of a Tour to New England Made by President Polk in June and July 1847.* Vanderbilt University Press.

Daniel, Dan. 1982. NACCCA (National Alumni of the CCC Association) Journal, Vol. 5, No. 3. (7900 Sudley Road, Suite 413, Manassas, VA 22110-2874.)

Dorrell, F.A. 1982. The expanding role of the forestry consultant in USDA-Forest Service Programs. The Consultant 27:4.

Drucker, Peter. 1989. *New Realities* Harper & Row Publ.

Fechner, Robert. 1939. My hopes for the CCC. American Forests, April 1939.

Gallagher, Hugh Gregory. 1990. *FDR's Splendid Deception* Dodd, Mead & Co.
Greeley, William. 1951. *Forests and Men.* Doubleday & Company.
Hawes, Austin F. 1936. The C.C.C. as an agency for stand improvement. Journal of Forestry 34, Vol. 7, (July 1936).
Holland, Kenneth & Frank Ernest Hill. 1942. *Youth in the CCC.* Publ. by American Council on Education, Washington. Reprint (1974) by Arno Press, NY.
Lacy, Leslie Alexander. 1976. *The Soil Soldiers* Chilton Book Company.
McEntee, James J. 1941. Now They Are Men. National Home Library Foundation.
McEntee, James J. 1942. The CCC at Work. A Story of 2,500,000 Young Men. United States Government Printing Office.
Merrill, Perry M. 1981. *Roosevelt's Forest Army.* Published by Perry H. Merrill, Elm Street, Montpelier, Vermont 05602.
Mitroff, Ian I. and Warren Bennis. 1989. *The Unreality Industry* A Birch Lane Press Book published by Carol Publishing Group.
Nixon, Edgar B. (ed.). 1957. *Franklin D. Roosevelt & Conservation.* United States Government Printing Office. Franklin D. Roosevelt Library.
O'Brien, Howard. 1983. Telephone conversation 1/4/83. Tel: 916-322-4676. California Department of Forestry, 1416 9th Street, Sacramento, CA 95814.
Salmond, John A. 1967. *The Civilian Conservation Corps,* 1933-1942. Duke University Press.
Sanders, Burton. Chief of Police, Northfield, Vermont 05663. Personal conversation.
Sitkoff, Harvard. 1985. *The New Deal Fifty Years Later.* Temple University Press.
Strauss, William and Neil Howe. 1991. *Generations: The history of America's Future 1584-2069.* William Morrow Publ.
Taylor, George Rogers. 1971. *The Turner Thesis.* D.C. Heath & Company.
Thorpe, Lloyd. 1972. *Men to Match the Mountains.* Printed for the author by Craftsman and Met Press, Seattle, Washington 98109. (Also available from The Forest History Society.)
Unknown. 1935 Approx. Possibly some reader can help me out. It has been many years but as I remember, the Judge was from Washington State (see last sentence in my paper).

Chapter 4 NATIONAL SERVICE AND ATTEMPTS TO REACTIVATE THE CCC

One of the earlier youth back-to-nature movements had swept through Europe between 1897 and 1914. Youth hiked and camped through fields and forests with mandolins, guitars, and the most informal clothing. This was the youth-led Wandervogel movement (Koch 1977). Unlike the CCC where the Director, Robert Fechner, resisted all attempts to broaden the scope of activities, including military training, the Wandervogel youth energy was ensnared by the German General Staff. Most of the youth died in Flanders.

The Moral Equivalent of War, a thesis written by Professor William James in 1912, advocated conscripting whole age classes of youth for a period of service to the community. The Moral Equivalent of War has come to mean 'National Service' with some schools of thought believing that such service should be mandatory, whereas other thinking is that any such program should be voluntary, but with irresistible incentives which eventually might become compelling. At any point in time there are numerous bills in Congress calling for National Service. In October 1989 there were eight such proposals in Congress. Some would cease all federal higher education assistance and divert these funds to those youth who had served their nation for one year or more, in the military, conservation work, or medical relief.

President Franklin Delano Roosevelt had read the Moral Equivalent of War, and had met Professor William James, but he could not see any connection or relationship with that theory and his Civilian Conservation Corps (Nixon,1957; Vol. 1, pp 209-210). Furthermore, the CCC had no implied, nor stated, public service obligation on the part of the enrollees. It would be wrong to use the CCC as an example of the success that might be attained by National Service. The CCC was a unique program. It was not National Service.

The CCC inadvertently became a social experiment in that it caused the first great mixing of America's ethnic groups. College graduates did not enroll in the CCC until late in the program when Professor Eugen Rosenstock Huessy of Dartmouth College encouraged one recent Harvard graduate (Frank Davidson) to enroll in the CCC in order to better understand the other part of America's population. Davidson eventually became a special investigator for the CCC.

At the same time, Professor Huessy was able to have a CCC camp at Sharon, Vermont designated as an experimental camp for testing the concept of National Service. They formed a non-profit foundation which could take ownership of land until rehabilitation was completed. The rehabilitated property would be sold and the funds used to acquire other run-down properties needing rehabilitation. Projects were begun. However, a few weeks later (January 20, 1941) the Boston Globe wrote that Professor Huessy had worked with German youth programs before coming to America and Dartmouth. The Nation's newspapers picked up the story.

Professor Huessy maintained that he had worked with German youth programs, but that he had left Germany when Hitler took over. (Huessy 1977). Senator Aiken came to the defense of Camp William James (as the camp had been named), but Congress withdrew the funding and Mc Entee willingly closed the camp a brief three weeks after it had started.

For the past twenty years proponents of National Service have coordinated their efforts through the National Service Secretariat, Inc. (5140 Sherier Pl., N.W., Washington, D.C. 20016, Tel. 202-244-5828.) The Director is Don Eberly. They have published many National Service Newsletters. Their reports include Congressional proposals. The Congressional Budget Office (CBO) estimated the five-year cost at $13.1 billion in 1980. The Newsletters report on the many states and cities which have their own Conservation Corps (San Francisco, New York City, Minnesota, and Atlanta are among them).

CALIFORNIA'S CONSERVATION CAMPS

The CCC had been the dominant force for fighting forest fires. The discontinuance of the CCC, especially at a time when the Japanese were launching balloon-carried incendiary devices to ignite our western forests, caused considerable concern. California reacted by employing inmates of correction centers as forest fire fighters. There were legal obstacles which had to be overcome. President Theodore Roosevelt, in his 1905 Presidential Executive order No. 325-A, forbade the use of prisoners on national forests, national parks and all other federal lands. A legal solution was found (Thorpe 1972).

The California Department of Corrections, the Department of the Youth Authority, and the Division of Forestry (Department of Conservation) have combined penal reform and environmental protection objectives with some success. During the past forty years the program has experienced expansions and contractions along with successes and setbacks. Obviously the program has generally been successful just on the basis it has continued this long. There have been escapes but they have been relatively few and rarely occur in times of emergency. The inmates have an excellent record of firefighting and providing other emergency services. However, there apparently has been no documented evidence concerning the long-range influence on the behavior of the former inmates.

In early 1983 California had 1,824 adults in 22 conservation camps;

600 youth in 8 conservation camps; and 220 adults in a program jointly run with two county jail systems. California has studied the correction center work-incentive laws of other states and has evolved their own law with which the Division of Forestry, at least, is very happy (O'Brien 1983) Few other states, if any, have had continuing success with such programs.

THE 1919 LABOR DEPARTMENT'S PAPER

In 1919 the Labor Department published a paper by Benton MacKaye: "Employment and Natural Resources — Possibilities of making new opportunities for employment through the settlement and development of agriculture and forest lands, and other resources." It is likely that MacKaye, a highly educated forester, was aware of Professor William James' (Harvard University) "Moral Equivalent of War" thesis. Benton MacKaye was the founder of our world-renowned Appalachian Trail (Chapter 5).

THE YOUTH CONSERVATION CORPS (YCC)

The prosperity that ensued following World War II nullified the need to reactivate the CCC. Congressional hearings on reactivation commenced in 1950. But, it was not until 1971 that President Nixon approved the Youth Conservation Corps (YCC) which continues on a small scale into the 1990's.

Section 1 of the YCC enabling legislation is entitled "POLICY AND PURPOSE". The paragraph concludes:

> Accordingly, it is the purpose of this Act to further the development and maintenance of the natural resources of the United States by the youth, upon whom will fall the ultimate responsibility for maintaining and managing these resources for the American people.

Strangely, the administrators of the program, guided by the Social Research Institute at the University of Michigan, found eight objectives of the YCC. The development of a work ethic was subordinated to a questionable environmental awareness program (Armstrong 1977). Nevertheless the YCC attained some measure of success and a favorable and lasting impact is being made on many young participants.

The YCC was established as a summer program for youth from 14 to 18 years of age. There have been both residential and non-residential camps. Some of the camps have been all boys but most have been both boys and girls. Initially camps varied in size from 24 to 50 youth. Camps have been on both federal and state lands. There have been far more applicants than could be accommodated. In the northeast the summer is divided into two sessions in order to accommodate a larger number. Youth selection methods varied from interviews to a lottery.

The Department of Forestry at the University of Vermont was assigned a research project examining the conservation accomplishments of the YCC. They had observers at a number of camps from Maine to California in 1972 and 1973. The observers were instructed to cooperate with camp leaders in every possible way in addition to procuring research data. (Once again, note the cooperative rather than confrontational approach.) Hence, the observers were very well received. Many served their camp in supervisory and administrative roles. Some of the YCC projects were a continuation of the CCC projects such as thinning pine stands which had been planted by the CCC.

The research examined the rate of work for various categories in order to provide guidance to future camp leaders in project planning. For example: on forest trail construction it was found the average rate of accomplishment was 30 lineal feet per youth hour. Fifty percent of the time the rate would vary from 10 lineal feet to 70 lineal feet. They also examined the factors upon which accomplishments depend:

    Span of control.. crew size varied from 4 to 12
    Age of the youth varied from 14 to 18
    Percent of girls in the crew varied from 70% to zero
    Percent of the youth with a farm background
    Hours of previous experience in that type of work
    Elevation
    Climatical factors

Research results were published (Armstrong 1975). The background of crew leaders was not quantified, not anticipating so many of them would have no forestry background. This became such a problem in the later Young Adult Conservation Corps that the President of the Society of American Foresters wrote letters to the Forest Service and the Department of the Interior on the matter (Orell 1978).

The nature of many work projects was recreational, such as parking lots and camp grounds. This may have been related to the skills of the crew leaders. Some camps, particularly the ones on state lands, were well managed. The YCC continues to this date, but at a reduced level, and primarily with non-residential projects. The minimum age limit has been shifted upwards to 16.

THE YOUNG ADULT CONSERVATION CORPS (YACC)

There was considerable Congressional momentum in 1976 to reactivate the CCC to about 500,000 youth. (The CCC peak strength was 502,000 enrollees.) However, these measures failed and a far smaller Young Adult Conservation Corps (YACC) was approved by President Carter in 1977 (Armstrong 1977). This program was beset with so many objectives that work projects were generally of the make-work variety

(Armstrong 1978). The chairman of the Society of American Forester's task force studying reactivation of the CCC toured a number of YACC camps when the program started. It was disappointing to find many youth raking leaves. The YACC lasted only three years.

Since the 1950's no government program, the world over, has been successful (Drucker 1989: 12). As soon as governmental activity has more than one purpose it degenerates (Drucker 1989: 65).

Despite setbacks there are ongoing examples of forests building men. Since 1975 the people of Vermont have been burning more than a cord of wood annually for every man, woman and child. This replaced millions of gallons of OPEC oil. It has had a favorable effect on the state balance of trade. And, there has been a beneficial effect on the work ethic of many youth. A central Vermont police chief said "As I look over Northfield, I can tell you that the children of families who burn wood just don't get into trouble" (Sanders 1978).

The U.S. Forest Service is contracting a large percentage of their work to consulting foresters and others. One of the reasons is far greater efficiency. In 1981 contracts for tree planting on national forests totalled twenty million dollars. Consulting foresters were able to employ youth on a piece-work basis which provides a strong incentive. National forests can not employ youth on a piece-work basis. National forests are also contracting other operations including timber stand improvement (tsi), boundary marking, and forest inventory. Forestry consulting business is now viewed as a growth industry (Dorrell 1983). Contracts are providing opportunities for many Americans to continue the partnership with forests. Physically challenging forestry work continues to have a beneficial influence on the behavior of Americans.

The author's interest in these matters stems from a statement made decades ago by a Washington State judge. "In all of my years on the bench I have never encountered a delinquent youth who had a hobby of fishing" (Unknown. About 1935).

CURRENT STATUS OF YOUTH CONSERVATION PROGRAMS

As aforementioned, the YCC continues as a summer program. There are no federal year-around youth conservation programs in 1991. The State of California does have a program. So do several cities, at least one county (Marin, CA), and some foundations. Canada tried such a program in 1977. No other countries had such a program in 1977 (Armstrong 1977).

In April 1988 more than fifty states, cities, and counties operated conservation and service programs that enrolled nearly 50,000 youth and had a combined budget of $145 million. Thirty-seven of the fifty included "conservation" in their titles (Hendee 1990).

JUSTIFICATION FOR A NEW CCC

The Society of American Foresters' Task Force on Reactivation of the CCC established the following factors which justify conservation work (Armstrong 1979).

1. There are many unemployed youth, particularly in the large cities.
2. The backlog of conservation work on government-managed forests is at least 1.8 million man years.
3. The needed conservation work is labor intensive, and will remain so even in the electronic age.
4. Work can be started with a minimum of planning time.
5. The cost and the volume of work are increasing every year.
6. The most essential work is associated with increasing timber production including: reforestation; timber stand improvement; timber-type conversion; thinning existing stands; and forest fire pre-suppression.
7. The CCC is evidence that such programs can succeed. The large volume of work accomplished by the CCC was eclipsed by values associated with strengthening human resources.

Obstacles which would detract from, or even stop, a youth conservation program, at the federal level, in the present era include:

1. Most of the work is in remote areas which are too distant for daily travel from the youths' homes. Residential camps would be required.
2. There would be very high costs associated with the program primarily because of organized labor's insistence on minimum wage plus room and board for residential camps (Biomeller 1977).
3. Child-labor laws do not allow youth under age 18 to use power tools nor engage in any dangerous activity such as forest-fire suppression.
4. The National Environmental Policy Act would require an Environmental Impact Statement for every residential camp, and also for every major project the occupants of the camp might ever construct. This facet would cause at least one year delay even if there were no challenges from local residents.
5. If the youth did live at home and were picked up by bus at local population centers daily, the law requires full pay for travel time.
6. Large construction, such as a residential camp, would have to be constructed by union labor at prevailing wages.

7. Most of the necessary work is seasonal in nature.
8. Mayors of big cities are not supportive of programs which would remove large numbers of youth from their cities (Gibson 1977).
9. Costs associated with a compulsory national service program would be as high as most any penal system.

CONCLUSIONS:

The foregoing justification, for reactivation of the CCC, applies at the federal, state or local level. Local level could mean county, city, or town. The foregoing obstacles primarily apply at the federal level, including the case where any federal money is involved. There are states, counties and cities which have youth conservation programs. The trend is in this direction. When there is no federal participation, the costs can be lower, environmental impact statements may not be required, and work can be located within commuting distance. If camps are to be constructed it might be possible to use the youth for this work without objection by organized labor. The mayors of big cities support conservation work provided it is in their city (Gibson 1977). It seems that federal youth conservation program legislation, and/or management, becomes beset with so many objectives, which are interjected by special-interest groups, that conservation work is relegated to a minor position. Lobbyists are not as well organized at some state capitols.

LITERATURE CITED

Armstrong, Frank H. 1975. Civilian Conservation Corps revival. J. For. Vol. 73, No. 6:15-16.

Armstrong, Frank H. 1977. Correspondence with embassies. For example, Dr. Hinrich Wachhorst, First Secretary Agricultural and Forestry Affairs of the Embassy of the Federal Republic of Germany (8/25/77) "The answer to your question, whether the Federal Republic of Germany has a national program for employing youth in forestry work or not, is definitely no." Armstrong, Frank H. 1977. Youth programs in conservation. J. For. Vol.75: 786-788.

Armstrong, Frank H. 1979. Final report of the task force on the reactivation of the CCC. Journal of Forestry Vol. 77, No 7:450.

Biomeller, Andy (AFL-CIO legislative director) 1977. Personal discussion.

Dammann, J. C. and R. A. Andrews. 1979. Economies in fuel wood supply firms in New Hampshire. Research Report no. 76, New Hampshire Agricultural Research Station.

Dorrell, F. A. 1982. The expanding role of the forestry consultant in USDA Forest Service programs. The Consultant Vol 27, No. 4.

Drucker, Peter. 1989. *New Realities* Harper & Row Publishers. Gibson, Kenneth A. (Mayor of Newark and and President of U.S. Conference of Mayors) 1977. Personal conversation at a U.S. Senate Committee February 3, 1977.

Hendee, John C. 1979. My Chance. Journal of Forestry Vol.88, No.8.
Huessy, Hans. 1977. Personnal discussion with son of Professor Huessy.
O'brien, Howard. 1983. Telephone Conversation 1/4/83. Tel 916 322 4676. California Dept. of Forestry, 1416 9th St., Sacramento, CA 95814.
Orell, B. L., President of S.A.F. 1978. Circulation of YACC vacancy announcements. J. For. Vol. 76, No. 9:621
Preiss, Jack J. 1978. *Camp William James*. Argo Books, Norwich, Vermont
Sanders, Burton. Chief of Police, Northfield, VT. Personal Conversation.
Thorpe, Lloyd. 1972. *Men to Match the Mountains*. Printed for the author by Craftsman and Met Press, Seattle, Washington 98109. Also available from The Forest History Society, Durham, N.C.
Weeks, Christopher. 1972. *Job Corps*. Little, Brown & Co., Boston

Chapter 5 OUR THREE CONSERVATION ERAS

There have been three distinct eras, in our national history, where millions of Americans have taken action to ward off damage to our natural environment. There will be a fourth, and even a fifth. They may occur in your lifetime. You may be the person who instigates such a movement.

Rather than focusing on history it is more meaningful for civic leaders to focus on:

1. the instigation, or causes, of each of the three movements.
2. identify the leaders and their motivation.
3. the strategy, or courses of action, they pursued.
4. the reasons for the fading of the movements.

President Lincoln was in office from 1861 to 1865. Sanford Gifford painted Twilight on Hunter Mountain in 1866 (Terra Museum of American Art, Chicago, Illinois). It portrays the Civil War era far better than mere words. It is one of the most disturbing works of the 19th Century. There is a stark and depressing image of ruin. The stump filled clearing is in a depression that replicates, in reverse, the shape of the majestic mountain above. The giant hemlock is a painful reminder of the once-virgin forest. The landscape was painted for James Pinchot who later named his eldest son after the artist. Gifford Pinchot was the first American to graduate from a forestry school.

Timothy O'Sullivan, who worked with Mathew Brady in photographing the Civil War, and afterwards in photographing the western wilderness, stated that Twilight on Hunter Mountain had a striking similarity to his photograph at Gettysburg, entitled "A Harvest of Death". O'Sullivan's photography, of the primeval western wilderness, is duly acclaimed to be among the finest in early photographic art.

When the Civil War ended, our western migration soared. New towns and cities seemed to spring up overnight. We had a cross-continental railroad in the same decade. These were all voracious users of wood. American lumbermen had moved from Maine westward to the Lake States. Their philosophy was cut the timber out and move on to new forests with no thought of forest management under sustained yield. The lumbermen in the Lake States were frequently the offspring of eastern lumber families. The soaring demand for wood, which accompanied the new wave of western migration, gave them even greater impetus.

George Perkins Marsh was U. S. ambassador to Italy at the time. He had grown up in central Vermont and gone on to a most remarkable career, indubitably based on little fear of hard work and diligent study. Marsh had studied at Dartmouth College, taught at Norwich University, and was a lawyer. He had been been a manufacturer, an editor, a legislator, a U.S. Congressman, Ambassador to Turkey, one of the co-founders of the Smithsonian Institute, and he was fluent in 20 languages.

Over the years he had been apalled at the widespread clearing of timberland, and the degradation of the water quality. And so in 1864 he published a book entitled *Man and Nature,* which became known as the "Fountain Head of the First Conservation era". The book has also been called the most consequential message ever delivered by a Vermonter. Marsh's book was translated into many languages. In 1866 it was printed in Russian and had a positive effect on the Russian conservation movement (Weiner 1986;p. 7).

Man and Nature is a scholarly scientific treatise on the influence, and physiology of woodlands and waters. Many years later another book was to instigate the third conservation era.

Forestry problems at that time were primarily devastation of forests by lumber barons, who after all, were simply performing in accord with accepted ethics, and devastating forest fires. The fires consumed thousands of square miles of old-growth forest, and also killed many people. More than a thousand people had been killed in Peshtigo, Wisconsin by one wildfire.

The American Forestry Assn (AFA) was founded in 1875 in response to these developments. Their stated objectives were to protect existing forests from unnecessary waste, and to encourage the propagation of useful trees. Note that neither of these goals precluded lumbering. The first president of the of the AFA was a physician as were many of the members. In 1977, Jim Craig, editor of their publication, *American Forests,* stated that physicians still constituted their largest membership block. Recently, one county forester reported 61 timberland-owning physicians plus 5 timberland owning veterinarians (Hall, 1991). There has been a love relationship between physicians and forests for more than one century.

Forestry commissions were appointed in many states in the 1880's. Arbor Day, a day for tree planting by Americans was instituted. Arboretums were established.

Congress became concerned. They appointed a commission to study our future wood consumption and supply. And most important, Congress empowered the President to withdraw lands from our Public Domain to be held as forest reserves. The land west of the thirteen original states, Kentucky, Tennessee (and Vermont, the fourteenth state) was generally considered Public Domain all of which was to eventually be in private ownership. This withdrawal concept meant that some of those lands would not be open to private ownership, but would be held by the federal government. President Harrison responded by withdrawing 13 million acres. President Cleveland doubled that. President Theodore Roosevelt more than trebled that. All the while opposition was intensifying. Westerners wanted those lands available for private ownership.

The matter was aggravated by some of the lands having significant minerals. Mining jobs hinged on keeping these lands open for use. Opposition increased to the point that Congress had to stop further withdrawals in most western states.

President Theodore Roosevelt was in office. Congress knew that he would veto such legislation. Hence, Congress attached an amendment, precluding further withdrawals in 13 western state, onto the all important appropriations bill. It was sent to the President. What would you have done as President?

Well, the President decided to sign the bill in a few days, and in the interim hastily withdrew millions of additional acres from the Public Domain in those specific states. The ensuing uproar did not phase President Roosevelt. Remember these forest reserves. They will be important to our Chapter 8, where we will find the reserves became our western national forests.

Tree planting became a craze in this era of 1865 until 1910. Rural youth planted trees in abandoned pastures and meadows. Today, many of these are sawtimber size and adding to our wonderful wood surplus. Tree planting books sold like hotcakes. A few examples are:

The Forest Tree Planter's Manual, by Leonard B. Hodges, 1879, Minnesota State Forestry Association

Handbook of Tree Planting, by Nathaniel Egleston, Chief of Forestry Division, USDA. 1900. D. Appleton & Co.

A Primer of Forestry, by Gifford Pinchot, Forester. 1900. Government Printing Office.

You might watch for used book sales, particularly by town libraries. Some of these historical books can be had for peanuts. They have historical value for they each contributed to our current wood surplus.

John Minto of Oregon advocated family forest farms where families could earn their livlihood from forest products. The concept sounds great but stumpage (stumpage is the value or volume of standing trees) has been, too cheap. Today, some tree farmers do earn substantial money from their timber but very very few are entirely self-reliant.

Norway spruce (picea abies (L) Karst) was introduced into America long before the Great Crusade (as the first conservation era became known). Norway spruce played a major part in the Great Crusade. World-wide, Norway spruce and Scotch pine were the most planted species until the 1980's when they were surpassed by loblolly pine. Norway spruce is still the one tree that is planted in a wide variety of regions. It is native to central and northern Europe. Mature Norway spruce can be identified, from some distance, by the pendant branches. It seems that all of the branchlets are on the lower side of the main branches, and the branchlets dangle downwards. The large cylindrical cones, four to seven inches long, mature in one year. Many cones persist on the tree through the winter. Norway spruce has sharp pointed, needle-like leaves that are longer than other spruces. Older Norway spruce have roughened bark with reddish brown scales.

Norway spruce was introduced into the U.S. in our early history as an ornamental, "A bit of the old world" as viewed by immigrants. It became a status symbol for cemeteries and farmsteads, particularly after the 1876 Philadelphia Exposition. This was the height of the Great Crusade. A fabulous number of potted Norway spruce seedlings went as souvenirs. This might have been an entrepeneur or possibly they were tokens from the Prussian forestry exhibit. The Prussian forester in charge was a grandson of Baron Frederick von Steuben (General Washington's drillmaster at Valley Forge). These tokens may explain the similar-sized mature Norway spruce which grace the fronts of many farm and homesteads across the northeast.

In early years of this century many Norway spruce were planted by various state forestry departments, forest industry, individuals and families. Many of the planted trees died but some survive. Generally they don't regenerate naturally because they have been displaced too far from their native habitat. However, there are exceptions where natural regeneration is underway. The wood is suitable for pulp and paper. It is not a valuable wood. The greatest value of Norway spruce in America is for ornamental and memorial use. The white pine weevil can be problematic. It gets into the terminal bud of the top leader, killing the leader, and causing a distorted tree. Generally, Norway spruce is one of the easiest trees to grow. Potted small trees can be brought indoors for the Christmas season and replanted, in a prepared hole in January, and still survive.

It is not an exceptionally large tree. Trees that are 100 feet tall and three or four feet in diameter can be found in many localities. The American Champion, at Durham, New Hampshire (Mrs. Mamie Marty), is 108 feet tall and a whopping 15.5 feet in diameter. Trees slow down height growth in their old age to the point where it is imperceptible. They continue growing in diameter as long as they live. Annual diameter growth of old trees is usually far smaller than the same trees grew at a younger age.

Examples of the use of Norway spruce as memorials abound. The Bishop Hill Spruce Grove in Illinois was planted in 1849 around the mass grave of cholera victims who were migrating westward. Fairfield Cemetery at Newman, Illinois has a large stately Norway spruce which a local family planted in 1855 by the grave of a baby who died while the family was travelling west by Conestoga wagon. North of Middle Amana, Iowa the Amana spruce grove was planted in 1855 by a German religious group.

The first conservation era became known as *THE GREAT CRUSADE*. The withdrawal of timber reserves from the Public Domain was confrontational. Other accomplishments were cooperative with very little, if any, opposition. Dominant accomplishments included:

1. Our western national forests were withdrawn from the Public Domain.
2. Forest fire losses were greatly reduced.
3. Millions of trees were planted.
4. Millions of ardent conservationists evolved.
5. Forestry courses were taught at prominent universities
6. Forestry degree programs were established.
7. Forestry was taught in many grammar schools.
8. Lumber barons considered forest management.

President Theodore Roosevelt and his close associate, forester Gifford Pinchot, were very much a part of the Great Crusade. President Roosevelt was recognized as a scholar, a naturalist, and a man of marked intellectual attainment (Burton 1988). He was an authority on big game. He was a Republican until he instigated the Bull Moose political party in his later years.

It all faded away in the first decade of this century, because the American people had confidence that the President, and his associates, would see that our natural resources were protected. The ending of the Great Crusade was climaxed in 1914 when the Dean of American Novelists, Hamlin Garland, (Funk & Wagnalls,1979 ed.), wrote *The Forester's Daughter* (Published by Harper Bros.). Berea McFarlane really ran the national forest on behalf of her father who was the official supervisor. They were both very good people. And then Wayland Norcross entered the scene. He was a Yale chemistry graduate, and the son of a wealthy lumberman, who was in Colorado for his health. He became motivated and joined the Forest Service as a ranger. Berea and Wayland were providing custodial management of the national forest, against the depredations of the local farmers and ranchers. The Forest Service people were heroic. This was the feeling of America at the time. Berea is a role model for women forestry students.

There were overflows of the Great Crusade. The Save the Redwoods League began acquiring California coastal redwoods in 1918. They wanted no federal government participation. They simply purchased redwood stands from lumbermen at fair price and then arranged to protect them. (The non-confrontational approach.) Today, these stands are a part of our Redwood National Park and California State Parks. The Nation shifted gears in 1917 to 1918 for World War I. Important forestry wartime developments will be discussed in later chapters.

In 1921 forester Benton MacKaye proposed a foot trail across the mountainous regions of the eastern seaboard from Maine to Georgia. It became known as the Appalachian Trail. The trail is 2,160 miles long, following the ridge line through 14 states. Governors, legislators, and other civic leaders of these states should be knowledgeable of the trail. It is the longest known footpath in the world. The trail traverses 8 national forests, 6 units of the National Park Service, more than 60 state forests and parks, and until recently through numerous non-industrial private forests and industry's forests.

The Appalachian Trail Conference, headquartered at Harpers Ferry, West Virginia, coordinates maintenance and other activity of the member clubs. By 1970 developmental pressures were forcing the trail roadside in some locations. Congress, on request of the Conference, granted $90 million to the National Park Service (NPS) to purchase easements, or the land as necessary, to provide protection for the trail into perpetuity. Congress was assured there would be little ongoing cost because maintenance of the trail would continue as a gigantic volunteer effort. By 1990 the NPS had concluded legal agreements to provide protection for 97% of the trail. The remaining acquisitions are difficult cases. It may be many years before we reach 100 percent. Fortunately, timberland prices were depressed during the primary acquisition period and hence this is one program which nearly remained within the original authorization. The agreement between the Conference and the NPS, whereby the Conference will manage and maintain a trail through government (NPS) owned lands, is an historic precedent. The volunteerism differs markedly from other governmental volunteer programs because in this case the volunteer is his/her own boss.

Other overflows of the Great Crusade included the remarkably successful 1920's mass-education program by the American Forestry Association (AFA). The AFA was rightfully concerned about the large number of incendiary forest fires throughout the southland. Many newly established pine plantations were destroyed. Hence, teams of foresters travelled through the South with a motion picture projector, and the film "Bad Burning Bill". The film showings were well publicized. This was generally the first opportunity for people in the rural south to see a motion picture. They flocked to see the film, shown in rural schools, churches, and meeting halls. Bad Burning Bill, with his black cape and hood, was the perfect villain. The southerners never forgot the message. Arson fires continue to some extent but they are not what they were.

In 1924 our first wilderness area was established in the Gila National Forest (New Mexico), thanks to certain early foresters. In 1925 there were five more wilderness areas.

THE NEW DEAL AND THE SECOND CONSERVATION ERA

The second great conservation era began when a forester became president. It was known as the New Deal Conservation Era. In earlier chapters we discussed the prevalence of sapling stands in the northeast, worn-out cottonfields in the south, and dust storms in the midwest during the 1930's. Erosion was serious in many locations. Natural tree regeneration was not adequate. Tree planting was needed. We have discussed the work of the CCC, but the Works Project Adminstration (WPA), and the Public Works Administration (PWA) also planted trees and did conservation work.

Federal funds were made available for state acquisition of forests and parks. Acquisition of our eastern national forests moved ahead under full steam. Forest industry intensified their forest acquisition and their forest management. Stream fish stocking accelerated. Automobile travel to national parks replaced railroad travel and in so doing made parks available to thousands of Americans, who otherwise might never have had the opportunity.

Possibly the greatest good from the New Deal Conservation Era came from the number of ardent conservationists who were encouraged by presidential leadership. CCC enrollees, upon returning home carried the conservation message to younger sisters and brothers, cousins, uncles, aunts, and parents. Forestry school enrollments soared, although many youth had to defer forestry education until after the war.

President Franklin D. Roosevelt accomplished conservation attainments by cooperation and not confrontation. When the courts eventually questioned use of the CCC for shelterbelt plantings on private lands most of the planting had been done. In response to the courts the President simply switched the work to the PWA, until that also was challenged. When use of the PWA was questioned by the courts, the President switched the tree planting to the WPA. Certainly the President cooperated with organized labor, the educators who wanted a teacher at each CCC camp, and with big business by providing them with consumers and the National Recovery Act (NRA).

The American Forestry Association began their continuing trail riders of the wilderness trips in the 1930's. These horseback trips include a different encampment each night.

The Day of Infamy brought the second conservation era to a close. The lights went out all over the world. Smokestacks belched. Americans, both men and women, went to war. Enormous quantities of wood were consumed. There was concern about the devastation of our timberlands but American timberland owners intensified their growth of wood and our western national forests substantially increased their timber sales.

THE THIRD CONSERVATION ERA

Rachel Carson's book *Silent Spring* (1962) was the fountainhead of our third conservation movement. Americans responded to her message and elected strong conservation advocates to Congress especially in 1963-1964. Our National Environmental Policy Act is responsible for a new national policy on protecting our environment, the creation of the Council on Environmental Quality, and the requirement for Environmental Impact Statements (EIS).

The May 1977 issue of American Forests magazine was critical of the EIS program because of its unforseen growth. There were 650 lawsuits in the first three years. Tens of thousands of EIS writers were at work. Seventy federal agencies were writing EIS, some in-house and others under contract. The third conservation era has been confrontational.

Other developments in the third conservation era included expansion of our wilderness areas. They now encompass more than 85 million acres. Many of these are in Alaska. Most of the wilderness areas in the lower 48 states are on national forests.

West coast states enacted forest practices acts, in the 1970's, which are state regulation of forest management on private lands. Other states enacted Right-to-farm legislation, which assured farmers and timberland owners of the right to conduct normal operations without fear of a law suit. Most states have laws which protect landowners, who make their lands available for public recreation, from lawsuits beyond the normal responsibilities that a landowner has to any trespasser. Property owners do have the responsibility to protect even trespassers from the dangers of vicious dogs, bulls, explosives etc.

In recent years the third conservation era has shifted gears to local government where there are increasing regulations regards subdivision, zoning, wetlands protection, and sanitary waste.

THE REFORESTATION TAX INCENTIVE

The Internal Revenue Service generally requires reforestation costs be added to the basis and recovered decades later when the trees are merchantable. Logically, it would seem, that where reforestation is done to re-establish a stand of trees following logging, reforestation costs could be merged with logging costs and deducted from the sale price of the harvested timber. However, this is not allowed. In 1980 Congress did approve the *REFORESTATION TAX INCENTIVE OF 1980*. This incentive is also included in the 1986 Tax Laws.

Essentially this provision allows a ten percent tax credit for reforestation costs in the tax year they are incurred. It also allows a seven year amortization of the entire amount over an eight year period. This means that in the year of reforestation the owners may deduct 1/14th of the costs under adjustments to income thus reducing adjusted gross income; 1/7th of the costs for the next six years; and 1/14th in the final year. *There is a $10,000 annual limit.* This limit excludes large corporations which are spending hundreds of thousands of dollars annually.

The reforestation tax incentive is for NIPF owners. The $10,000 annual limitation precludes its use for most of forest industry's tree planting. Perhaps someday all tree planting costs will be recognized as costs of restoring natural resources following a timber harvest or even a natural calamity. This would be logical.

An example of the use of the incentive is explained in Appendix B. A NIPF owner invested $1,000 in reforestation for three consecutive years. Their total investment was $3,000. from which they would be able to recover $1,275. When the trees are eventually sold the NIPF owners will pay income taxes (long-term capital gains) on the price received. The example in Appendix B considers the time value of money, or compound interest.

Large-volume tree planting, such as by forest industry, has two significant disincentives.

1. The money invested in tree planting cannot be recovered until the planted trees are harvested, decades later. Even then, no additions are allowed for long-term inflation nor for the time value of money. Also, the amount recovered is linked to the income tax rate, or generally about 30 percent.
2. Trees are real estate. Pine tree plantations in the south, and Douglas fir plantations in the Pacific Northwest, are valuable real estate. Thus tree planting escalates the assessed value of the forest resulting in higher taxes. Property taxes are paid on the trees every year, and as the trees get larger the taxes are higher. On the other hand, clearcutting of all trees can dramatically lower property taxes.

Remarkably, forest industry and non-industrial private forest owners are planting about two billion trees per year. There are, and there have been, a few governmental incentive programs which have benefited a very small number of non-industrial owners. The vast majority of the plantings are not subsidized. There are absolutely no governmental price supports for forest products. There is no demand for price supports.

Tree planting entails a certain risk. A plantation lost to fire, disease, insects, or storm has no insurance coverage. If the loss is greater than ten percent of the owner's income they may recover some money from itemizing the casualty loss on their income tax.

The underlying reason for much of the planting is that forest industry must have wood raw material to supply their manufacturing plants.

SUMMARY: The third conservation era may still be underway, but indicators are that the scenario has shifted to state and local government. Forestry school enrollments plummeted in the late 1980's (discussion in Chapter 9). In any event there will be a fourth conservation era. It may differ in being world-wide, although there is evidence that the first three conservation eras also had world-wide implications. There is a 67 percent probability that the person who initiates the new era will be an accomplished writer, based on past conservation eras. There is also a probability that the new era will be marked by leadership which seems to accomplish far more than confrontational legislation.

Literature Cited
Burton, David H. 1988. *The Learned Presidency — Theodore Roosevelt, William Howard Taft, Woodrow Wilson.* Fairleigh Dickinson University Press.
Cutright, Paul Russell. 1983. *Theodore Roosevelt — The making of a conservationist.* University of Illinois Press.
Garland, Hamlin. 1914. *The Forester's Daughter.* Harper & Brothers.
Greene, Susan R. et al. 1985. How goes environmental regulation? Resources No. 81, Publ by Resources for the Future.
Hall, William P. 1991. Correspondence between the authors, and William P. Hall, Chittenden County Forester, Vermont.
Hodges, Leonard B. 1879. *The Forest Tree Planter's Manual.* Publ. by Minnesota State Forestry Assn., J.J. Lemon Book and Job Printer.

PART II.
AMERICAN TIMBERLAND OWNERSHIP

A window seat on a clear day over many parts of the nation discloses an ocean of green forest. Pick out any spot at random and focus on: Who owns it? What is the highest and best economic use of that acreage? Is the land open for public recreation? Is it part of our 85 million acres of designated wilderness? Is a logging operation in progress? Are the trees very large with sawtimber potential? Where is the nearest sawmill or pulp and paper mill? Would I want to own it if it were ever on the market? These are typical questions we will answer in Part II.

Part II will also introduce the subject of real estate because forests and standing trees are real estate (a class of property). Ownership of real estate constitutes real property. When trees are felled, the logs are personalty. Ownership of personalty constitutes personal property. The difference can be very meaningful. For example, assessments under some real estate tax laws include the standing tree value.

There are about 2.7 million licensed real estate people in the United States. Real estate brokers are generally independent business people who employ licensed real estate sales persons. The broker is the key person, who is usually acting in the role of an agent on behalf of sellers or buyers. Some brokers belong to the real estate boards and are classified as Realtors. Realtors are a subset of brokers.

Chapter 6 NON-INDUSTRIAL PRIVATE FORESTS (NIPF)

If you are focusing on one spot of timberland, from that window seat, the probability is that it is family or individually owned. Sixty percent of our timberland is owned by non-industrial private forest owners. There is considerable variance between states. In some states NIPF constitute more than 80 percent of the timberland. From your window seat the stone walls, old fence lines, tree blazes, and access roads are not evident but they are there. Parcel sizes vary from a few acres to several thousand. The probability is that, if your random spot is in one of the original thirteen states, Vermont, West Virginia, Kentucky, Tennessee, or Texas, where there was no public land survey, the parcel is about 100 acres. In the other states the parcel is likely to be some multiple of 40 acres. And, there is an 80 percent probability that this is the only parcel these owners have. There is a slightly greater than 80 percent probability of there being no structures on the parcel but I would wager the owners have good intentions to eventually build. They seldom ever get around to doing so. Now, in between these last few lines we can glean a profile of the typical owner. No, they are not rich. This is a frequently misunderstood facet so let's delve deeper into that and then continue to develop the typical owner profile. (Some of our cited literature will be incorporated into the text for obvious reasons.)

The motivating factor for forest ownership is that some people have aspirations to own land other than their home lot. Such persons usually have the determination to fulfill their aspirations by forfeiting other luxuries. The intuitive desire to own land may develop at an early age but the fulfillment of the desire is generally in middle age. There are exceptions. In 1975 an 11-year-old girl purchased a parcel of timberland at a tax sale in Roxbury, Vermont. She used a few hundred dollars from her school-savings account. This was full ownership in Fee and not a trust account. The Frederick Jackson Turner thesis of 1893, develops some of the motivating factors, although the prime theme is strengthening of our Democracy by the endurement of forest-frontier hardships. Other writers have stated that wealthy persons tend to invest in intangibles rather than real esate. Interestingly, this was recognized in early Vermont.

Even then there was criticism of professional people who owned little real estate but had excellent incomes. To answer this criticism, Vermont levied a "faculty tax" on such persons thereby attempting to relate their income to an equivalent amount of property. This faculty tax was used for over sixty years before it was abolished. (Andrew E. and Edith W. Nuquist 1966, Vermont State Government and Administration. Essex Publishing Company Inc.,p. 159. And Laws of 1779, p. 11, abolished by No. 16, of the Laws of 1847).

The word "faculty", as used in that era, referred to the possession of a great deal of knowledge as is the case of lawyers. The tax was imposed on lawyers and some tradespersons. Physicians were not included because then and now physicians frequently own timberland as well as other real estate (see Chapter 5).

Typically non-industrial private forest owners are not wealthy people This has been a heavily studied facet of ownership. For example:

Robert O. Sinclair, former Dean of the College of Agriculture at the University of Vermont, found the annual family income of non-local Vermont owners of Vermont land was less than $10,000 for 46 percent of the owners. (Robert O. Sinclair and Meyer, S.B. 1972. Nonresident ownership of property in Vermont. Bulletin 670, Agriculture Experiment Station, University of Vermont.)

An independent study found the 1973 family income for 45 percent of New Hampshire and Vermont forest-land owners to be less than $10,000. (Neal P. Kingsley and Birch, T.W. 1977. The Forest Land Owners of New Hampshire and Vermont. Forest Service Bulletin NE-51.)

Thirty-six percent of the 4,590 parcels of Vermont forests and associated lands, all larger than ten acres, sold for less than a total price of $8,000 between January 1975 and October 1977. (Frank H. Armstrong and Briggs, R.D. 1977. Valuation of Vermont Forests 1968-1977. Department of Forestry, University of Vermont.)

A 1975 Gallup Survey revealed 21.6 percent of Americans with family income less than $10,000 owned real estate other than their homes.

In Oregon the 1973 median family income of urban owners of forests in Western Oregon was $15,000. (Kent B. Downing et al. 1976. Urban owners of forests in western Oregon. OSU Research Paper 26.)

Thirty percent of the Pennsylvania forest owners, owning 29 percent of the acreage, had 1977 family incomes lower than $10,000. (Thomas W. Birch and Dennis, D.F. 1980. The forest land owners of Pennsylvania. Forest Service Resource Bulletin NE-66.)

In Louisiana one out of four small timber tract owners had 1973 family incomes of less than $4,000. (C.B. Marlin, 1974. Characteristics of owners of small timber tracts in Southwest Louisiana.(LSU Forestry Notes.)

Fifty-six percent of West Virginia forest owners had 1975 family incomes lower than $10,000. (Thomas W. Birch and Kingsley, N.P. 1978. The forest-land owners of West Virginia. Forest Service Resource Bulletin NE-59.)

In New Jersey 54 percent of the forest owners, owning 37 percent of the forest acreage, had 1972 family incomes under $10,000. (Neal P. Kingsley and Finley, J.C. 1975. The forest-land owners of New Jersey. Forest Service Resource Bulletin NE-39.)

And, in the prosperous state of Delaware 81 percent of the forest owners, owning 69 percent of the forest acreage, had 1972 family incomes lower than $10,000. (Neal P. Kingsley and Finley, J.C. 1975. The forest-land owners of Delaware. Forest Service Resource Bulletin NE-38.)

There is also growing evidence that owners of other classes of real estate are not rich. For example, it is reported that five percent of the nation's households own a second home. The range was from 4 percent of those with family incomes of $7,000 to $10,000 (1970 incomes) to 17 percent of those with incomes greater than $50,000 (1970 income). The median income of families owning a second home was $11,400. (Payne, Brian R. and Lloyd C. Irland. 1975. The second-home recreation market in the northeast. Bureau of Outdoor Recreation.)

From your window seat, that ocean of green doesn't reveal ownership objectives. They are diverse and multiple but included therein is the satisfaction of an early youth 'feel for the land.' Eventually the owner's goals will change and they will sell. Average length of ownership is 20 years, which is several times longer than most people live in one home. When they do sell they will probably provide the buyer with a short-term purchase-money mortgage.

Bequests of timberland are few because when owners become strapped for cash in their older age timberlands are usually the first asset liquified. Rising medical costs are offsetting any well-planned retirement annuities. Even when there are bequests the heirs probably have no desire to own timberland and so the property is soon on the market. Tax laws are also a stimulus for immediate sale by heirs for there is usually no tax to pay on the sale. The heirs' basis is the market value of the property at the time of inheritance.

You may envision firewood production on that spot of forest you are focusing on. Yes, our knowledgeable Secretary of Energy has warned us of another energy crisis. There will be renewed market demands for firewood and energy wood. The number of public utilities, generating electricity from wood, has been growing rapidly in northern New England as well as in other regions. These utilities consume large volumes of very low grade wood. They can even use trees that have been dead for a year or more. Generally, the loggers stockpile whole trees in huge piles, and then when there is sufficient volume, a whole-tree chipper is brought onto the site. These machines can take in trees up to 21 inches in diameter, convert them to chips, and blow them into a large van which hauls the chips to the electric generating plant. When chips are produced in the woods from whole trees the chips are mixed with bark, twigs, and even leaves. The chips are suitable for burning as hog-fuel, (to generate electricity) but they cannot be used for pulp and paper. That useage requires clean wood chips. The value of firewood and energy wood are trivial compared to sawlogs and veneer logs.

A Twenty-One-Year Case History of Timberland Price Reporting

The following case history demonstrates the cyclic nature of timberland prices.

Timberland prices are independent of price trends for other classes of real estate. Residential, commercial, industrial, and vacation property prices appear to have peaked, and even declined in the early 1990's. Farmland prices peaked in 1981, then dipped until 1990 when they appear to be on the rise again. Timberland prices are another matter.

There have been, and there will continue to be, land booms where timberland price increases exceed general inflation. In between these periods timberland price changes don't maintain pace with inflation. Timberland owners are generally reluctant to sell for less than they paid (in current dollars) and so the length of average ownership becomes significantly longer during the down periods. Stumpage price changes generally don't dominate the factors which affect timberland prices, except in the Pacific Northwest and parts of the South. Stumpage prices, unlike timberland prices, are widely reported. Our Vermont case history is the only well-documented portrayal of the cyclic nature of timberland values that we know of.

Vermont has required the reporting of prices paid in real estate transfers since 1968. It is one of the few states which has a two-decade record of real estate transfer price reporting. The voluminous files of the Vermont Department of Taxes (upwards of 22,000 property transfers per year of all classes of real estate) were not computerized until 1985, and even then not in a format useable for this continuing study until 1988. Now, a private venture is providing price information on all classes of real estate for a small fee. The time lapse from the closing date until the availability of the data is about three months.

Vermont is 77 percent forested and 81 percent of the forest is owned by non-industrial private owners. Seventy-three percent of the privately owned timberland is in parcels larger than 100 acres, and 46 percent is in parcels larger than 250 acres (Widmann & Birch 1985).

Vermont, like much of the nation, experienced a surge in demand from several years before 1968 through 1973. Much of the demand was from from those who envisioned subdivision, and speculative vacation-home development (Armstrong 1974). Annual price increases averaged 12 percent (Armstrong 1975). The 1973 peak was followed by lower prices, except for two short-lived peaks in 1981 and 1983, as measured in current dollars. However, since late 1986 prices have increased exponentially and activity has increased. This is contrary to other real estate.

Reasons forest prices did not maintain pace with inflation from 1973 until 1985 include: high interest rates made other investments more attractive; forest property taxes soared compared to other real estate taxes, and other costs; timberland could not be depreciated and hence was not an income tax shelter; there were increasing state and local regulations impinging on forest management;Canadian softwood lumber imports soared during that era and dampened softwood lumber prices; the long-projected timber famine vanished from the horizon; and the mid 1970's vacation-home market turned out to be far smaller than had been anticipated.

Reasons for the 1986-1990 increased prices, and volume transferred, are: the October 1987 stock market decline motivated some investors to diversify; highly publicized sales of timberland by forest industry at bargain prices attracted considerable interest, bringing new investors into the market; the volume of the timber growing stock on much of the Vermont forest has been increasing at 3 to 4 percent annually (and the value even more) while prices for forest properties remained level from 1974 until 1986. Thus by 1985 many parcels were priced less than the value of the timber theron; population demographics indicate, that all else being equal, the demand for vacation properties, that are sufficiently large to provide solitude, should increase through 1995 (Armstrong 1987); Vermont, and many other states, have, in recent years, enacted laws that provide for taxation of managed forest properties under current-use criteria (which is a far lower tax); the generally favorable economic conditions, accompanied by repeated warnings of inflation from the Federal Reserve Board, stimulates investment in tangibles.

Studies have focused on forests and associated real estate that have no structures of any significant value. Tables 3, 4, and 5 have not been corrected for inflation. Appraisers do not routinely adjust prices for inflation as economists do. They should not because to do so would imply that timberlands are expected to maintain pace with overall inflation which they just don't do every year. A timberland appraiser, in adjusting comparable sales, would not adjust comparable sales prices for inflation. The appraiser would adjust for time only where the appraiser had evidence timberland parcels in that region did increase, or decrease, during the period spanned by the various comparable sales. Incidentally, the property owners' basis (land and timber accounts) must be in current dollars. They cannot be indexed for inflation.

There was a precipitous drop in activity commencing in 1974, as indicated in the last column of Table 3. Actually the drop commenced in May 1974 when a Vermont Land Gains Tax became effective. However, the reduced activity cannot be blamed entirely on the Land Gains Tax because if that were the case there would have been revived activity six years later (the tax is only imposed on sales within six years of acquisition). Furthermore there was reduced activity and prices for timberland in other states commencing in 1974. Note that in the late 1970's, while farmland prices were escalating, timberland prices were depressed. Farmland and timberland prices are established by entirely different factors. By the early 1980's there were millions of acres of timberland on the market. There would have been more if prices were better.

The extent of Vermont forest subdivisions and mergers has not been studied. When a person buys two or more parcels at the same time lawyers usually merge this acquisition into one deed. Whether or not mergers are offsetting subdivisions is not known. Column 3 of table 3 doesn't evidence whether average timberland parcel sizes are becoming smaller, or larger.

In the introduction, we have seen that forest acreage, in many northeastern states continues to expand.

Table 3. Vermont Timberland Parcels 250 Acres and Larger Transferred

Year	Average price per acre	Average parcel size	Parcels
	Dollars	Acres	No.
1968	121	446	100
1969	124	472	87
1970	149	415	79
1971	166	559	74
1972	178	526	93
1973	248	384	80
1974	193	615	23
1975	168	486	33

1976	209	763	40
1977	197	451	28
1978	213	549	28
1979	181	885	42
1980	219	687	46
1981	307	507	33
1982	205	765	18
1983	286	677	35
1984	201	743	22
1985	241	250	14
1986	304	347	48
1987	296	485	32
1988	368	735	53
1989	691	419	56
1990	632	481	25

Table 4. *Vermont Timberland Parcels 100 TO 249 Acres Transferred*

Year	Average price per acre	Average parcel size	Parcels
	Dollars	Acres	No.
1983	312	143	123
1984	337	136	60
1985	377	144	79
1986	392	140	198
1987	509	145	240
1988	572	146	232
1989	1066	147	227
1990	1005	148	128

Table 5. *Small Parcels of Vermont Timberland Transferred*

Year		Average price per acre	Average parcel size	Parcels
		Dollars	Acres	No.
1984	75-99 acres	399	83	31
1985	75-99 acres	541	83	45
1986	75-99 acres	556	84	47
1987	75-99 acres	658	85	114
1988	75-99 acres	716	85	111
1989	75-99 acres	1687	84	112
1990	75-99 acres	1569	86	49
1988	50-74 acres	713	59	216
1989	50-74 acres	1697	59	211
1990	50-74 acres	1650	61	98

1988	25-49 acres	1029	35	412
1989	25-49 acres	2691	34	394
1990	25-49 acres	1984	34	233

This report has given average prices for the specific line item. There are 4,222 timberland sales in this report. The range of prices within the parcels on any line is large because of varying qualities of the parcels. Other studies (Armstrong 1974) (Turner 1989) have examined various qualities of parcels along with correlation of prices.

There has never been any federal price reporting of timberlands.

All income, including real estate sales, is reportable to the Internal Revenue Service and in many cases to the state department of taxes, but this information is not available to the public. Real estate appraisers generally need information on consummated sales of comparable properties to support their findings. There are a dozen states where real estate prices are confidential, or at least there are no provisions for making the prices avaialable to the public (Table 6). Montana does require reporting of real estate prices on realty transfers, but the same law stipulates the confidentiality of price.

Prior to 1968 federal revenue stamps were required for real estate transfers. Since the expiration of the federal tax some states have adopted a state deed-stamp tax on real estate transfers (Table 6). The counting of deed stamps can provide general price information. However, appraisers report the counting of deed stamps is not a reliable method of determining price paid, especially where the information may have to be defended in a court of law. Problems include:

1. Applying the correct rate which may vary with the date. New Hampshire, for example, has had seven rates in the past 21 years.
2. Some states vary the rate by the class of ownership.
3. The value reported under some deed-stamp laws is on the honor system. In Florida, for one example, it is possible to buy more documentary stamps than required for the purchase price in order to mislead appraisers as to the actual price. Recently a state-wide Grand Jury, investigating spurious state acquisition of coastal properties, recommended penalties be imposed for providing false information on real estate transaction documents. In other states, such as North Carolina, the willful and knowing failure to pay the correct amount of excise tax constitutes a misdemeanor by their criminal laws.
4. There are states where the merchantable timber can be sold without any report. Then the land and unmerchantable timber can be sold separately to the same parties and duly reported.

5. Loan assumptions may not be duly reflected by the deed stamps in Georgia, North Carolina, and possibly other states.

Some states require a property transfer return inorder to document a property transfer tax (Table 6). By and large reported prices appear to be accurate as have been verified by comparison with advertising.

There are also states which require an affidavit of prices paid unless the deed specifies the full price (Table 6). Louisiana differs from the other 49 states in that much of their law is derived from the Napoleonic Code. Prices paid for real estate in Louisiana are clearly stated in the deed.

Multiple listing services in all states, report prices of completed sales, along with property descriptions, to their membership. However, multiple listing services are more prevalent in the residential real estate market than in the timberland market. Appraisers generally find parties, involved in real estate transfers, are cooperative in furnishing price information when the need for comparable sales is duly explained to them. (Remember this one, for there is some probability that during your lifetime a real estate appraiser will ask you about one of your recent sales or acquisitions of real estate. The appraiser is not prying into your business in any way that may harm you financially. Our system of a free market economy hinges on your cooperation if possible.)

Table 6. *State Confidentiality on Real Estate Prices*

Confidential Matter	Deed Stamp Law	Property Transfer Return	Affidavit or Deed
Alaska	California	Arizona	Alabama
Idaho	Colorado	Maine	Arkansas
Indiana	Connecticut	Nebraska	Florida
Michigan(2)	Delaware	Pennsylvania	Hawaii
Missouri	Georgia	Vermont	Kansas
Kansas	Illinois	Wisconsin(3)	Lousiana
Mississippi	Iowa	(Not public info)	Minnesota
Montana	Kentucky	New Jersey	
New Mexico	Maryland	Oregon	
North Dakota	Massachusetts	South Carolina	
Texas	Nevada	South Dakota	
Utah	New Hampshire	Tennessee	
Wyoming	New York	Virginia(2)	
	North Carolina		
	Oklahoma		
	Ohio		
	Rhode Island		
	Washington		
	West Virginia		

(Original compilation by the authors, who have used varying sources)

1. The Virginia grantor's tax, of $1 per $1,000, is listed at the end of each deed recorded. The sale price is also recorded in the circuit court clerk's receipt book which is available to the public. This is considered to be correct information by appraisers.
2. In Michigan the transfer affidavit containing both price and transfer stamps, is not available to the public.
3. Wisconsin's property transfer return is considered a tax document and as such is not available to the public. Social security numbers are also on the property transfer return which is one more reason for confidentiality. Wisconsin also has a deed stamp law at $3 per thousand value. The determination of price paid for a specific parcel by counting the deed stamps can be done at the county court house. However, locating any class of comparables (such as 40-acre woodlots) is not very feasible. Township assessors may, or may not, have the time to assist appraisers in locating comparables.

In economic theory a perfectly competitive market relies on several conditions, one of which is knowledge of prices by all parties involved in the market. The public has benefited from past Vermont price reporting. Real estate appraisers have relied on these reports to direct them towards comparable sales. More recently, price information on real estate sales is public information in most states. Nevertheless, scarcely a day goes by when some timberland owner sells out for a price far below the market. Many are evincing self reliance in not seeking expert advice on current prices. It is usually a costly move. On the other hand, there are timberland buyers who are constantly alert for these numerous underpriced parcels.

Timberland ownership is extremely illiquid, meaning that it can take many years to sell a property. Owners who are financially prepared for such delays are frequently rewarded with annual returns on investment that can range from 25 percent and upwards.

End of Case History

Total land area in the United States is about 2.3 billion acres. Thirty-one percent is forest (737 million acres). And two-thirds of the forest is timberland (482 million acres). Non-commercial forest is the difference (255 million acres). Non-commercial forest is generally at a northerly latitude or high elevation where trees don't grow well, or else is reserved from timbering by law. Most non-commercial forest is in governmental ownership.

Sixty-percent of timberland is in non-industrial private forest ownerships. There are about 7.8 million timberland owners. However, this includes those who own parcels as small as one acre.

Table 7. *Owners of Three Hundred and Thirty Million acres of N.I.P.F.*

Parcel size	Owners	Percent of the Acreage
1-10 acres	5,500,000	2
10-50 acres	1,200,000	10.5
50 + acres	1,100.000	87.5

Most ownerships are two people (husband and wife). A few are individuals. And some are multiple owners with an undivided interest. These range upwards from two and three people who have gone together and purchased a property each with an undivided interest. One may own 30 percent but it is not known which part of the property they own.

Legal classes of ownership include:

Tenanacy by the Entirety where a husband and wife own the property jointly. Should one of them die, the other immediately takes over full ownership without proceeding through probate.

Tenacy in Common is where two or more persons own an undivided interest in a property. The percentage would be specified in land records and could vary between the owners. Should one of them die their share is assigned to their heirs.

Joint Tenancy is the same as tenancy in common except the survivor takes all, as in the case of Tenancy by the Entirety. This might be a useful ownership for a father and daughter.

Children can own real estate, but there would be complications should the child wish to sell before reaching the age of 18.

From your window seat you cannot see stone walls, old fence lines, and blazed trails that delineate ownerships. They are very real, however. If we could go back a century you would have seen many of them. It is frequently not possible to walk more than a half mile in most any straight line without encountering a land line. You may not recognize it if you don't know what you are looking for.

Some owners mark their land lines with paint, others blaze a line, and some do both. Others rely on old fences now deeply imbedded in trees. Some lines are not marked. A few owners map their property. Many properties have been legally surveyed, but not all. Some lands-records offices (at county or town level) have tax maps where the owner of most every parcel can be located. Then there are others, especially in the east, where the owner is the only person who knows the location of the property. And, there are even owners, who have been duly paying property taxes for decades but don't know where their land lines are.

About 20 percent of parcels in the northeast have structures on them which increase annual property taxes. Some owners avoid these taxes by using a recreation vehicle (RV) and motor out to their property on weekends. Vacation homes in the northeast are referred to as camps which are generally modest seasonal homes. However, they can verge on palatial. Camps are

a way of life in New England and other regions. They have great value to the owners and to society.
1. A safe secluded location for parties and reunions.
2. Hunting camp activity allied with reinforcing family way of life.
3. Introducing children to rural life.
4. Provide farmers with some income and friendly part-time neighbors.

One of our basic freedoms in the United States is the right to mobility. This includes the right of U.S. citizens to own property in any state. Only Nebraska has restrictions on foreign ownership. Frequently N.I.P.F. owners eventually relocate to their forest for retirement.

Posting of lands against trespass varies greatly between regions. In a 1988 Virginia study, 27 percent of privately owned lands were open to the public for hunting without necessarily being acquainted with the owner (Bowman 1989). Nearly all timberlands in northern New England are not posted. This means that the public can enjoy these properties for hunting and other non-motorized recreation. Many states have laws which specify that where owners make their lands available to the public they incur no greater liability than they would owe to a trespasser. Yes, property owners have the duty of protecting even trespassers against intentional harm or attacks by vicious dogs.

Fields are interspersed with forests. Eventually, fields become forested unless measures are taken to maintain the openings. Fields have great value to wildlife.

Timberland ownership has few parallels with farm ownership. Farm ownership is generally longer; there are more bequests of farms; farm purchases can usually be financed by banks; and boom periods for farmlands do not usually coincide with timberland booms.

The reasons for owning timberlands are complex and evasive. Querying owners can evince one response today and a totally different response a week later. Nevertheless the evidence, which has been compiled by numerous studies, does give us a good indication.
1. Eighty percent of owners have only one parcel.
2. The average period of ownership is about 20 years.
3. Timberland is not a tax shelter because land and timber cannot be depreciated by Internal Revenue Service rules.
4. Value increases are sporadic. They can be associated with boom periods or by a change in products, as happens when a stand of trees increases from pole sized to sawtimber size.
5. There are few bequests, and even then the inheritor will probably sell. Incidentally, the inheritor establishes the basis as the value of the property at the time of inheritance. Hence, if they sell at that time there is no gain to be taxed.
6. Few parcels of timberland are given as gifts. The recipient is required to carry over the basis of the donor which could very well mean a large taxable gain.

7. Most parcels are mortgage free. But generally owners still are carrying a mortgage on their home.
8. When owners are strapped for cash (possibly old-age medical costs), the timberland is usually the first thing they liquidate.
9. The propensity to sell standing timber varies. When timberland prices are depressed, and owners are reluctant to sell for less than they paid, they are quite likely to sell some standing timber.
10. Frequently, it is the wife (widow) who ends up with the timberland for women do live longer.

One ownership objective has been to have an investment with inflationary safe guards. However, this was not upheld in the 1974 to 1985 period. Certainly many owners could be considered speculators. Speculating in real estate is not un-American.

> From the earliest days of settlement to the present, probably nothing has been more characteristic of the American than his persistent efforts to dabble in real estate and to gamble on their increase in value. (Nuquist and Nuquist 1966; p. 480)

Vermont, with a population of 535,000, has about 26,000 real estate transfers per year. Of course, many are residential properties. This is an annual transfer for every 21 people.

Charles Royster is prominent in historical writing. In his book *Light Horse Harry Lee* (p. 176) he names America's most experienced active, and successful land speculator, General George Washington. Light Horse Harry Lee, a dynamic general of the American Revolution, and father of General Robert E. Lee, did so poorly in timberland speculation that he served time in debtor's prison.

Most timberland acquisitions have been two-party affairs, meaning no real estate agent was involved. However, there are some dedicated real estate brokers who derive a great deal of their satisfaction from helping people satisfy their needs. There are far easier ways of earning commissions than from selling timberland where the prices (and commissions) are low and the time to show a property can be long.

Banks are reluctant to finance timberlands except for preferred customers. Some insurance companies finance very large acquisitions. But by and large most timberland acquisitions are financed by the seller who provides a purchase money mortgage to the buyer. The time period is very short, frequently only five years. The down payment is generally 25 percent.

Timberland fire, storm, insect, and disease insurance is not available. But, the loss probability is really quite slim, and even then salvage timber cuts may recuperate much of the loss. Most owners do have liability insurance under their regular homeowner's policy. If this is not the case, the costs are quite low.

Revenues are dominantly from timber sales or sale of the entire property. A few owners do well with maple syrup sales. In parts of the south the sale of baled pine needles for garden mulch is lucrative. Hunting leases have trivial value but, on the other hand, leasing of hunting rights to a responsible club can include excellent timber theft protection for absentee owners. Other recreational leases may aggravate your liability.

Some states, including Vermont, have adopted acceptable forest management practices (AMP's) for logging. They have the force of law. Compliance is enforced through penalties for violations. AMP's are designed to prevent discharges of mud, petroleum products, and woody debris into stream, ponds, and wetlands. Forest owners can place responsibility on loggers by a properly worded timber sale contract. Note, if there is no stream or other water body, there can be no violation. By and large, loggers are responsible people.

West coast states have state regulation of forest management practices. Eastern foresters have been striving to stave off state governmental regulation of forest management by seeing to it that logging is done in a manner that will not adversely affect the environment. Extension foresters, in many states, have conducted schools for loggers. Obviously loggers are trying to do well for voluntary attendance at these schools has been superb. Loggers are indispensable to forestry. We are fortunate in having people who do want to work very hard in all types of weather. We will continue to have loggers only as long as they can make a profit.

The Capper Volstead Act of 1920 authorized agricultural and forestry cooperatives in certain situations and exempted these co-ops from provisions of the Sherman Ant-trust Act. Within a few years there were thousands of forestry cooperatives. Some owned a sawmill; others shared logging equipment; but most shared marketing expertise. Most of these have fallen by the wayside. Only a dozen or so remain today. There are none at all in the northeast. Forestry cooperatives have been successful in Scandanavia and so numerous studies have been conducted to determine the reasons for their failure in the U.S.A. The leading reasons seems to be that management has failed, and NIPF owners are individualistic in America. Management failures seem to stem from lack of financial incentives when managers are on a salary.

TIMBERLAND PRODUCTIVITY IN AMERICA

Sixty years ago Congress charged the USFS with the responsibility of periodically assessing the status of timber in each state. Congress also charged the USFS with responsibility for long-range prediction of market demands for timber. Congress felt that if so very much of our timberland was in private ownership it would be well to advise owners on future demands (which they assume will increase) so that investors will intensify their operations. Thus, more timber would be available to the market and prices would be lower than otherwise.

NIPF objectives are varied and probably dominated by non-wood considerations. However, objectives of government differ. There is nothing wrong with this. Although wood production of our timberlands has im-

proved immensely in the past hundred years, our timberlands are still not near potential. NIPF are doing no worse than other ownership classes, but they do own so much timberland that most government programs have been N.I.P.F. oriented. Governmental programs include:
1. Agricultural Cooperative Program (cost sharing of management).
2. Forestry Incentive Program (cost sharing of management practices).
3. Reforestation tax incentive which was discussed in Chapter 5.
4. Long-term capital gains treatment of timberland earnings was in effect from 1943 to 1987 (this will be dicsussed in the next Chapter).
5. Soil bank program of the 1950's which paid farmers for planting trees on former crop land.
6. Conservation Reserve Program where landowners enter into contracts to retire highly erodible cropland. The goal is to have 12.5 percent of that land planted to trees.

Some NIPF are Tree Farms. That topic will be discussed in the next chapter.

SUMMARY: Civic leaders, especially attorneys and bankers, should readily recognize situations where clients are paying too much for timberlands. They should not be surprised by low income families aspiring to timberland ownership. They should understand that most buyers of small parcels will never build theron although their intents are otherwise. Primarily they should understand the recurring 'land boom' phenomena along with the causes. And, it is all right for government to be concerned about stimulating timber productivity on NIPF whereas owners may have other objectives. That ocean of green you are viewing from your window seat should be far more meaningful to you now.

LITERATURE CITED

Armstrong, F. H. 1974. Valuation of amenity forests. The Consultant Vol. 19 (1):13-19

Armstrong, F. H. 1975. Valuation of Vermont forests 1968-1974. Dep. For., Univ. of Vermont, 30 pages.

Armstrong, F. H. 1987. Is timber the highest and best economic use of Vermont forest properties? Northern Journal of Applied Forestry 4 (4).

Armstrong, F. H., and R. D. Briggs. 1977. Valuation of Vermont forests 1968-1977. Dep. For., Univ. of Vermont.

Bowman, Jim. 1989. Private land: Is it all locked up? Virginia Wildlife. Vol. 50, No. 11:17-21.

Crowell, John B. 1982. What is the proper role of the federal government in support of forestry on private lands? J. of the Assn. of Consulting Foresters, Vol. 27, No.4;68-71.

Royster, Charles. 1981. *Light Horse Harry Lee.* Alfred A. Knopf, NY.

Vicary, Bret. 1989. Northern forest lands study—Executive Summary, The Irland Group, Forestry Consultants, Augusta, Maine.

Chapter 7 FOREST INDUSTRY

Your chosen spot of timberland has some possibility of being owned by forest industry for they own about 13 percent of our timberland. If you are observing a coniferous stand (softwoods) the probability is somewhat greater than 13 percent. Forest industry was acquiring available large parcels of timberland until about 1974. Then the situation changed and many corporations, not only stopped acquisition but, commenced divesting themselves of timberland. For example, forest industry owned 14 percent of Vermont's timberland in 1973. Ten years later this had declined to 9 percent (with N.I.P.F. increasing accordingly). There was more timberland on the market in the 1980's than at any time this century, and much of it was forest industry's. If prices had been better there would have been more than the estimated nine million acres that was on the active market.

Our primary teaching points for this chapter are:
1. Forest industry does own some excellent timberlands and, although they only own 13 percent of our timberlands, they produce 34 percent of our sawtimber.
2. Forest industry needs wood to keep their manufacturing plants going. Generally they would prefer not to own any forests at all, and procure wood from NIPF and public forests.
3. The shortage of woods labor has forced mechanization of many of industry's logging operations. They are really not certain as to whether it is more economical or not, but it solves their problem.
4. Public relations is important to forest industry.
5. Their timber management is efficient, intensive, and scientific, far eclipsing timber management by NIPF and government.
6. Subsets of forest industry, such as the poles and piling industry, tend to be regional.
7. Forests industry has been quick to adapt to changing technology.
8. There are no governmental forest product price supports comparable to the agricultural sector. No one is advocating them.
9. There is no forest damage insurance to cover losses from forest fires, volcanoes, storms, insects or disease. Most authorities believe the actual risk is minimal.

Forest industry is generally defined as corporations which own some timberland and manufacture forest products such as lumber. Some definitions include a minimum acreage. The ranking of the corporations is sometimes by value, or volume, of the timber growing stock they own (Weyerhaeuser is first by this approach). We could also rank the corporations by the acreage they own. The first four in 1990 were:

1. Georgia Pacific   8.5 million acres
2. International Paper Company   7.1 "   "
3. Champion-International & St. Regis.   6.2 "   "
4. Weyerhaeuser   5.9 "   "

During the era, when there was the spector of a timber famine on the horizon, forest industry was buying timberland whenever large parcels (500 acres and up) came on the market. However, by 1974 a series of developments changed the situation and forest industry slowed their acquisition and even divested themselves of some timberlands.

Developments were topped by wood becoming surplus to our needs, even though the U.S. was consuming all-time record volumes of wood by 1987. Much of the wood was from Canada, but even if Canadians reverted to their normal export volumes the spector of a timber famine had disappeared by 1983. High interest rates aggravated borrowing for needed manufacturing plant environmental controls, and it was easier to liquidate timberland than borrow funds. Property taxes on timberlands soared, compared to other classes of property and costs. Timber and land cannot be depreciated for income tax purposes. Hence forest ownership was not a tax shelter. (However, timber depletion allowances can be used to recover actual investment money, but only when there is a timber harvest.) Increasing state regulation of forest management on private lands (particularly on the west coast) was aggravating costs. This was all topped off in the mid-80's by the recision of the long-term capital gains favorable tax rate on timberland earnings. However, there is strong support from President Bush, and some members of Congress, in 1992 for restoration of the favorable rates.

Another viewpoint, which well summarizes much of the foregoing, was that corporate accountants, with their general accepted accounting procedures, had convinced the corporate officers to sell some of their timberlands. It was unfortunate for industry that these developments climaxed at a time when the market for timberlands was depressed. On the other hand those who acquired the divested timberlands derived some bargains. These included state and federal government, but primarily NIPF owners.

Some corporations, recognizing depressed timberland prices, developed the concept of limited partnerships. In effect purchasers earn the value of the harvested timber for a specified number of years. The corporation is the general partner. Limited timberland partnerships have also been created by investment firms.

> The $20 million Hutton Southern Timber Partners I...has lost money six years out of seven... Yet Hutton earned $3.9 million in fees and distributions. "A Limited partnership isn't a timber investment so much as an annuity whose income stream is dependent on timber prices and good behavior by the general partner (Hayes 1989).

Corporations which divested themselves of considerable timberland during the low-price era probably already regret their action. The regrets may be considerably greater if forecasts of increased demand for forest products turn out to be correct.

FOREST INDUSTRY   89

The McSweeney-McNary Act of 1928 charged the Secretary of agriculture with responsibility for forecasting requirements for forest products. Congress anticipated that accurate forecasts would motivate investment, thus increasing supply, along with lower prices than would otherwise be the case. The United States Forest Service (USFS) responded to this charge with early 1930-period estimates of future requirements. These estimates were based on forecasts of future population, income, employment, production technology, individual preferences, and other pertinent factors. A current analysis of these forecasts shows they were low, particularly so in pulpwood estimates.

The Forest Service has been fifty-year forecasting for, after all, growing timber is a long-range project. Naturally predictions of demand and supply of timber in the year 2040 are risky to say the least. Nevertheless, the Forest Service has refined their methods and invests considerable talent in these forecasts.

Our ensuing discussion will primarily focus on cubic feet of wood as opposed to board feet. One board foot is a piece of wood that is one-inch thick and one foot square. Board feet are primarily used for lumber. Cubic feet, on the other hand, would additionally include pulp (raw material for paper), paper, lumber, and other wood products.

The volume of softwoods (coniferous species) used in the United States is about double the volume of hardwoods (deciduous species). For example, in 1986 softwood consumption was 13.7 billion cubic feet while hardwood consumption was 6.9 billion cubic feet. When we consider the volume of timber growing stock in cubic feet on all U.S. timberlands, softwoods comprise 57 percent and hardwoods 43 percent. Net volume of growing stock in cubic feet is the volume of useable trees that are one foot or larger at the stump and includes volume to a four-inch top diameter.

In 1989 the Forest Service published a draft compilation of the analysis of the timber situation in the United States 1989-2040 in two parts (Haynes 1989). Part I is the current resource and use situation. Part II is the future resource situation.

HISTORICAL DATA AND PROJECTIONS TO 2040

Acreage in timberland in the United States is expected to decline from 480.7 million acres in 1986 to 459.7 million acres in 2040 (Haynes 1989). This is an insignificant annual decline of about 8/100ths of one percent. Volume of timber growing stock, and annual increment on the average acre have been increasing dramatically since at least 1952.

YEAR	TIMBERLAND ACRES	AVERAGE GROWING STOCK IN CU. FT.	AVERAGE ANNUAL INCREMENT IN CU. FT.
1952	449,331,900	1208	27.9
1962	509,380,100	1272	32.8
1970	496,404,100	1371	39.8
1976	482,485,900	1474	44.9
1987	483,100,000	1562	46.3

Most of the 1962 to 1976 decline in timberland acreage was a result of creating wilderness areas, which by definition cannot be timberland.

HISTORICAL AND PROJECTED STATISTICS

Billions cubic feet

	Hardwood		Softwood
1987 growing stock	304.938		449.975
2040 " "	370.003*		432.439*
1987 annual increment	9.653		12.734
1987 removals (harvests)	5.176		11.864
1986 imports (combined softwood & hardwood)		4.4	
1986 exports " " "		2.3	
1952 historical consumption	2.7	8.1	
1970 " "	2.9		
1986 " "	6.5		9.5
2000 projected consumption	8.3		14.1
2020 " "	10.2		14.3
2040 " "	10.5		16.8
			18.5

(Haynes 1989)

*growing stock in the year 2040 had to be re-estimated by the author because Alaska and Hawaii were not included in the reference. However, at this time Alaska contributes 10.29% of our softwood and 2.5% of our hardwood growing stock. It was assumed this proportion would continue.

NOTE: removals, plus imports less exports should equal the apparent consumption. They don't quite balance in the above because they are different years. The largest increases in consumption are expected to be in paper, paperboard, and panels (panels include 4 ft. by 8 ft. sheets of plywood, chip board etc.). We do import low valued forest products and export high valued forest products so the dollar imbalance is less than the volume imbalance. In 1975, 1980 and 1988 the value of forest product imports was essentially equal to the value of exports. In 1989 and 1990 the value of forest products exports was greater than the value of imports.

NOTE: Hardwood growing stock, and annual increment, have been increasing for many years because much of our hardwood forests had been cleared for agriculture and then reforested. Softwood growing stock is an altogether different matter. In 1950 most softwood growing stock was in old-growth forests in the Pacific Northwest. These were never cleared for agriculture. Annual increment on old growth forests is low. However, as they are eventually cut there is a resurgence in the annual increment but at the expense of depletion of growing stock. Softwood growing stock losses in the Pacific Northwest have been offset by significant increases in growing stock in our southern pine lands. There also has been more tree planting, in each of the recent years, than the Civilian Conservation Corps (CCC) accomplished in ten years. Most of this tree planting has been in the South and the Pacific Northwest.

Successfully planted forests can eventually have very large volumes of growing timber because there is no waste space. These fully-stocked forests will be very meaningful to future consumption. The first two or three decades of a planted forest show no measurable growing stock. Eventually the trees reach measurable size and then appear in our Forest Service statistics. Then decades later they reach merchantable size and have a marked influence on forest statistics.

Large volumes of growing stock per acre are important to the people who admire amenity values in fully-stocked older-aged forests. Large annual increments per acre are important to consumption of timber products if we support the sustained-yield philosophy. It does take wood to make wood (TWTMW), and it is true that a larger growing stock per acre will generally result in larger annual increments, but only up to a certain point. Eventually the older forest will commence to experience a decline in annual increment even though growing stock volume may continue to increase at a diminished rate. (NOTE: this paragraph may be the most important in this chapter.)

HARDWOODS 1987-2040

Hardwood growing stock inventories in 1987 were 304.938 billion cubic feet whereas the 1977 growing stock totaled 244 billion cubic feet. Our hardwood growing stock has been increasing at nearly two percent every year (compounded) for at least the past 24 years. Seventy percent of hardwood forests are in non-industrial private ownership. Eleven percent is owned by forest industry. The bulk of hardwood timber is in the East, roughly equally divided between the North and South. The annual increment is about three percent of the growing stock. Annual removals are about two percent of the growing stock.

Hardwood stumpage prices are projected to increase 267 percent by the year 2040, in 1986 dollars. This is a relative price increase of 1.8 percent annually. There will also be an assumed 4.34 percent annual increase in general price levels (Haynes 1989). Hence stumpage that sold in 1986 for $100 per mbf will reputedly be selling (in current dollars) for $2,599 per m.b.f. in the year 2040.

$$\$100 \ (1.018*1.0434)^{54} = \$2,599$$

The U.S. Forest Service Forest Products Laboratory at Madison, Wisconsin reports past records of hardwood prices are not meaningful because they are not for a fixed mix of sawlog species, nor a constant quality. We are using species that were not used in the past (Skog 1982).

The 1978 Hardwood Market Report of lumber values has walnut in first place followed by cherry, ash, white oak, red oak, basswood, hard maple, soft maple, birch, hickory, yellow poplar, and beech in sequence (Wiant 1980). In northern New England red oak and ash are at the top with yellow birch coming in close in the 1990 market value.

The immediate outlook for large-sized (hardwood) sawtimber of preferred species such as white and red oak, black walnut, and black cherry is for very large increases in stumpage prices (Hair 1980).

It is assumed that residential use of wood fuels will increase from six million cords in 1976 to approximately 26 million cords in 2030. However, it is possible that demand will rise much beyond this projected level (Hair 1982).

SOFTWOODS 1987-2040

Forty-one percent of softwood growing stock is on national forests and 16 percent is on forest industry's timberland. Geographic distribution of softwood growing stock is: 66 percent in the west; 23 percent in the south; and 11 percent in the northeast.

Softwood lumber, which primarily is used for construction, had an average relative annual price increase of 1.8% from 1800 until 1970 (Duerr 1973, p. xv). Since 1970, prices in current dollars have been volatile but essentially have not increased. However, Forest Service forecasts are for large increases in market demand for both softwood and hardwood lumber. Based on that prediction the Forest Service anticipates a resumption of the upward movement of lumber prices. The following discussion simply documents this paragraph.

Stumpage is the raw material for lumber. Stumpage prices have experienced a similar pattern (plus a few years time lag) to lumber prices. There were positive annual relative stumpage price increases (meaning increases above average inflation) from at least 1910 until the late 1970's. Since then prices have stabilized. If anticipated demand develops there will be a resumption of the upward price movement for stumpage. Again, the following discussion is documentation for this statement.

Softwood stumpage relative price increases (above and beyond general inflation) to the year 2040 are given (Haynes 1989) in six regions. The author has modified the data in the reference to read as an annual percentage increase.

ANNUAL PERCENTAGE INCREASE

Northeast:	3.07%
South:	2.49%
Rocky Mountain	4.51%
Pacific NW	2.93%
Ponderosa pine subregion	2.83%
Pacific Southwest	2.77%

Between 1910 and 1970 relative prices of Douglas fir stumpage rose an average of 3.5 percent annually while southern pine stumpage increased about 3.2 percent annually (Hair 1973).

Sawtimber stumpage prices rose sharply from 1950 to 1977. Then they dropped, probably in recognition of our wood surplus. Expected stumpage shortages, due to national forests declines in allowable cut, have caused great variation in prices in recent years. The decline in allowable cut on national forests is to protect the spotted owl in the Pacific Northwest, and woodpeckers in the South.

Projections prepared by the Food and Agricultural Organization of the United Nations indicate world demand for wood fiber products will increase substantially in the decades ahead. U.S. manufacturers may find participation in international markets much more attractive than they have in the past (LeMaster 1978).

Forest industry doesn't relish the thought of steeply rising stumpage prices. They fear the public would switch to substitute materials and once the switch has been made it is difficult to reverse (Vaux 1973).

Canadian and American timber markets are so intertwined it is difficult to look at one without considering the other. This facet is especially important to foresters along the border such as in Maine. Lloyd Irland was a forestry professor at Yale. Currently he is a consulting forester in Maine.

The harvests projected by the USDA Forest Service cannot be met on a sustainable basis without a major commitment to intensified management. The Province of New Bunswick is in a serious timber supply situation, facing some regional shortages with respect to particular products in a time span of 15 to 25 years from now (Irland 1981).

Most Canadian forests are owned by provincial governments. Forest industry is Canada's largest commodity industry.

It is difficult to estimate, but 20 to 60 million acres (in Canada) are now inadequately stocked with trees, and this backlog is increasing at the rate of 500,000 acres annually (Bourchier 1982).

Housing is the dominant consumer of softwoods. In 1986 U.S. annual production of new housing units was 2,051,000. This was about the same as in 1985, 1984, 1983, and 1979. In 1986, 57 percent were single family; 31 percent were multi-family; and 12 percent mobile homes. Projections are for slowly declining housing starts with 1,892,000 in the year 2040. Sixty-six percent will be single family homes (Haynes 1989). (NOTE: 1990 and 1991 housing starts were low.)

Floor area of average single family homes has been increasing in the U.S. In 1950 the average was 1,150 square feet. In 1986 it was 1,825 square feet. Forest products used in the average 1986 single family home were 13 m.b.f. of lumber; 209 structural panels 4' X 8'; and 84 non-structural panels (Haynes 1989).

In 1982 there were 1,648,700 persons employed in U.S. forest products industry. Persons in timber harvesting were 80,900. The trend is towards fewer persons employed in the industry although production is increasing (Haynes 1989). (NOTE: employees have dropped to about 1.2 million in 1991.)

Lumber recovery from a typical log is projected to continue increasing. For example, in the Ponderosa pine subregion board feet lumber tally, per cubic feet, log scale in 1985 was 6.05. It is projected that this will be 7.50 in the year 2040 which reflects efficiency of computer operated sawmill headrig decisions and other technology (Haynes 1989).

PULPWOOD PRICES

Pulpwood (softwood and hardwood) stumpage prices have scarcely moved in decades. One reason is that pulp and paper plants now accept most any species of wood, whereas fifty or more years ago they only accepted certain softwoods. Another reason is the geographic distribution of pulp and paper mills generally means there is usually one buyer in a region and many sellers.

Our forest products mix in 1986 was 36 percent of the cubic feet of wood harvested went into lumber; 26 percent went into pulpwood; 23 percent was fuelwood; 8 percent was used for plywood and veneer; and the remaining

7 percent was for other products such as poles, piling, fenceposts, and cabin logs.

REGIONALIZATION

Large forest products corporations own timberland in many parts of the nation, but they have concentrated where forests are most productive.

MAINE: If your window seat is overlooking Maine, you are over forest in all probability. Perhaps you gain the impression that you are usually over one of 1,600 lakes, but water surface constitutes only 6.5 percent of the state. There is a 47 percent chance that your selected spot of forest is owned by forest industry. This is the highest percentage of any state. A great deal of Maine's forest is spruce-fir type. These are very tolerant species so there can be many stems per acre. Whereas the individual trees may not grow very fast, the total annual volume that is grown per acre can be very high, and even as high as in any region of the South. Spruce and fir are prized for pulpwood and so much of the industry is pulp and paper manufacturing. Lumber, plywood, and other products are produced. During the period 1970 through 1985 spruce budworm devastated some of Maine's spruce-fir forest. Much of this is being naturally replaced by aspen. The spruce budworm population took a nose dive and in 1986 the problem vanished until some future outbreak.

PACIFIC NORTHWEST: The timberlands that are west of the cascades, where they have ample rainfall, are highly productive. Old-growth stands had extremely high volumes per acre. Much of the sawtimber industry is there.

SOUTHERN ALABAMA: The region surrounding Mobile is ideal for longleaf pine, the best of the four southern pines. Slow-grown longleaf pine is prized for poles and piling and hence the industry is concentrated there. Logs must average six growth rings per inch or more to qualify for the poles and piling market. Slow grown conifers are stronger than fast grown. The reverse is true for many hardwoods. Fast grown hickory makes stronger baseball bats.

SOUTHEAST: In the 1930's, when technology devised a method of making paper from southern pines, forest industry gravitated into the region. The worn out cotton fields were able to produce pulpwood in 25 years or less. So, our southern pine pulp and paper industry is concentrated in South Carolina, Florida, Georgia, and Alabama.

LAKE STATE REGION: In the building boom, following the Civil War, forest industry moved into the Lake States and cut immense volumes of pine. Aspen, a pioneer species, followed many of those clearcuts and when technology devised paper production from aspen, and associated species, there developed a concentration of paper manufacturing plants in that region. The dominant pulpwood species in the Lake States is aspen.

SOUTH-CENTRAL: But our main case history is our south central region, eastern Texas, Louisiana, Arkansas, Mississippi—where there were truly magnificent stands of old-growth pine. This is the region where highly intensive forest management evolved that now eclipses silvicultural practice anywhere else in the world.

THE SOUTH'S FOURTH FOREST IS GROWING

There are many forest product companies which significantly contributed to economic development of this region. Some of the ones which we have personal knowledge of are the Urania Lumber Company, Crossett Lumber Company, Fordyce Lumber Company, and William Buchanan's Pinewood Lumber Company (later the Bodcaw Company). A composite synopsis of their development will simply be referred to as "The Company."

Immediately after the Civil War Congress enacted the Southern Homestead Act which intended to sell 47 million acres of public domain in Alabama, Arkansas, Florida, Louisiana, and Mississippi. Anyone who was not an ex-confederate could have 80 acres at very low cost. Ten years later the act was rescinded because private acquisition had been trivial. After repeal of the act, a flood of Northern and foreign speculators purchased large blocks from the government. Then responsible southerners commenced acquiring the land from the speculators (Mayor 1988). The new owners organized the Company and at the turn of the century constructed a large sawmill.

Many white farmers did purchase land and tried farming, but it didn't pay well and they had to seek other sources of income. This meant logging and sawmilling. Note in the many photos of the logging, and sawmilling, in this era the workers are generally white. A few employers, such as Buchanan, did employ African Americans for certain work such as in the mill-yard (Mayor 1988).

Clearcutting and railroad logging dominated the scene. The peak production year was 1909. The original Company philosophy was to cut out the timber and move onto other lands with no thought of forest management. Attempts were made to interest northern farmers in the cutover lands, but the farmers realized the soils were not good for agriculture. The harvested timber was all a part of the South's first forest. Timber cutting had begun as far back as 1608 in Virginia and thence progressed westward. A second-growth forest regenerated naturally in some locations and there were numerous plantings of southern pine.

About 1920 the Company realized there were no other lands to move on to. They only had sufficient reserve timber to supply their large sawmill for another decade. Much of the acreage they had cut twenty years earlier had naturally regenerated into pine and seemed to be growing very well. (But there were also vast tracts of stumps and grass). The logging foreman had been recommending truck logging instead of costly railroad logging. And the Company had heard a great deal about the new forest management. The decision was made to give it a try. A Yale forestry graduate was hired.

Paper was originally made from rags until late 1800's when wood was first used on a large scale. Initially the wood was spruce. Then in the 1920's technology found they could also use southern pines. The Company constructed a Kraft paper mill in 1937.

The sawmill and pulpmill consumed large volumes of wood, more than the Company could justifiably harvest from their own lands. Hence a wood procurement office was established. Generally, they would purchase standing timber (stumpage) from NIPF and arrange with independent contractors to cut it and deliver it to the mill.

In 1943 a change in the laws taxed all earnings from wood, regardless of how and why the wood was cut, at the long-term capital gains rate which was about half the normal income tax rate. Thus the earnings from the timberlands were taxed at a far lower rate than earnings from the mills. This reinforced the necessity of the woodlands division selling the wood to their own mills (on paper transactions) in order to enable proper accounting. This development had far-reaching effects. For one thing the woodlands manager now was able to procure the needed money for a tree nursery, new logging roads, intensified tree planting, and timber stand improvement measures.

World War II used vast quantities of wood as we discussed in Chapter 1. The Company's profits were very good. Generally, the last of the South's first forest was harvested and by this time the second growth (Second Forest) was being harvested.

Truck logging had replaced railroad logging. In fact, many of the former railroad beds were now roads. The company no longer employed logging crews for they used independent contractors to harvest their own lands as well as to procure wood from NIPF. They were also starting to procure wood from national forests by the independent contractor system. If a contractor had need for financing new equipment the Company was ready and willing to loan the funds. Forest industry pioneered the "unbundling concept" (subcontracting out certain operations) which is forecast to prevail during the 1990's in most other businesses.

For some of the more outlying regions concentration yards developed adjacent to railroad sidings. The independent yard operator dealt with the independent contractors, procured the wood, sorted the logs so they were destined for the highest paying market, loaded them on to railcars, and shipped them to the mill. The whole system is very efficient with built-in incentives.

The timber buyer frequently has primary concern about total volume and quality; then volume per acre; then distance; and lastly price. Market demand for wood can be highly volatile.

Incidentally, there are about 390 companies which manufacture paper in the United States. They consume about 57 million cords of wood plus 32 million cords of residue (clean chips and sawdust) per year. Alabama and Georgia lead the nation in paper and paperboard production. Our per capita consumption is 600 pounds of paper and is growing. Total consumption exceeds 200 million tons of paper and paperboard. We export about 50 million tons. And we import about half of our newsprint from Canada.

Newsprint accounts for 15.4% of our tonnage consumption

Printing & writing paper accounts for 26.1%

Other paper and paper board account for 58.5%

Shortly after World War II, when the woodlands manager requested more funds, management asked "What has been your return on past investments?" The woodlands manager calculated his return on investment (R.O.I) by dividing the value of the annnual harvest of timber by the land and timber account (book value). The land and timber account were the actual dollars expended for the initial acquisition back in the 1890's, plus additions due to planting costs less total depletion due to timber harvests. The book value (the denominator) was very low and so the R.O.I. was high. The woodlands manager felt good about that report. Then, the corporate accountant stated the denominator should not be book value, but market value. This approach would use a high denominator and the R.O.I. would be low.

The woodlands manager faced a dilemma because of the high cost of attaining an appraisal of current market value. The problem was solved when a number of corporations made offers to acquire the Company. They simply used the best offer as current market value.

The Company considered some very attractive acquisition offers that included payment by stock (which would not be taxable until cashed in); the Company would continue with the same personnel as it had in the past, but it would be a division of the larger corporation; and there was even a guarantee on the value of the large corporations stock one year after the merger. The company also considered the low R.O.I. their woodlands were earning and the high estate taxes that would be due if they continued as they were with only a few families owning the Company. They agreed to the merger.

NOTE: There were 424 friendly mergers of forest products firms in the period 1959 to 1970 (Le Master 1977).

The South's Second Forest (second growth) had been evolving as the first forest was cut. By 1968 the second forest had been largely cut, and a start was made on cutting the third forest. It is expected to last until the year 2000. The South's Fourth Forest is underway. It has been evolving since about 1968 when we started cutting the third forest.

About 1970, technology developed methods of manufacturing plywood from southern pines, the Company (now the Division) constructed a plywood plant to supplement their sawmill and their pulp and paper mill. In fact, a regional concentration of plywood plants evolved in the central south because plywood needs large high quality logs, and it was the central south that had them to support their sawtimber manufacturing. The decision was really made by the large corporations "Operations Research Team." This was a group of scientists who were well into mathematical solutions to real world problems. Their tools included linear programming, simulation, queuing theory, and sequencing.

Another development emanated from new interstate highways which sliced through corporate lands. The Division was cognizant of the financial opportunities that could be realized in constructing motels on their lands where there were exits from the interstate. The Division (and the owning corporation) were becoming a regional conglomerate. You might wonder about the ethics of benefiting from government highway construction, but before you condemn the Division, consider the opposite case. A company has had a motel on a state highway for many years. Business has been good. Now the local community is building a by-pass around the town which will veer off most of the traffic from ready access to the motel. Do they reimburse the motel owners for the lost revenues? No! Sometimes this is referred to as inverse condemnation but the motels owners lose out. You win some, and you lose some, that is business.

In less than a decade technology had developed chipboard, where any wood (even junk wood) can be chipped and then glued back together into panels that are 4 feet by 8 feet. They are used for construction. Generally, it is lighter in weight than plywood. This makes life easier for builders. Aspen makes very light weight chipboard. The Division added a chipboard plant to their conglomerate.

Wood procurement from NIPF and national forests is becoming ever more important for the Division with all of the new manufacturing plants. NIPF are the prime source, for they own 60 percent of the timberland. Wood procurement methods, from lands other than their own, now include:

1. Leasing of forests, commonly for 75 years.
2. Direct wood purchases from loggers who deliver to their mills.
3. Indirect wood purchases from concentration yards.
4. Acquisition of timber from other firms where it is favored by geographic ownership.
5. Stumpage bids for national forest timber sales.
6. Cooperative programs, where the Division has foresters contact NIPF owners and provide them with free forest management service in exchange for the right-of-first-refusal should the owners ever sell standing timber. Some of these cooperative programs include:
   A. Land Owner Assistance Program (LAP) by International Paper Co.
   B. Private Land Untilization Service (PLUS) by Union Camp.
   C. Tree Farm Family (TFF) by Weyerhaeuser Co.
   D. Cooperative Forest Management Plan (CFMP) by WestVaco.
   E. Tree Farm Cooperator Program (TFCP) by Champion—St. Regis.

The Association of Consulting Foresters (ACF), which provides similar services to NIPF owners, but for a fee, has questioned the ethics of these cooperative programs. For example, the ACF believes a corporate forester might steer the NIPF owners toward producing pulpwood if that is the company's need in the region. But, the owner might better be advised to produce sawtimber. It has been a healthy debate and corporate foresters are cautious about their business ethics.

Overall the relationship between NIPF owners and forest industry is excellent. Many NIPF owners are content in producing raw material. Industry would rather concentrate on manufacturing. Forest industry has been interested in acquiring large forest properties which appeared on the market, until recently. They never had an interest in acquiring typical NIPF because parcels are too small for effective administration. Neither party can afford to lose the other. Should a trend develop, whereby NIPF owners become reluctant to harvest trees (as is the case in Finland) industry will have problems.

Recent developments which may affect forest industry include:
1. Environmental pressures are driving up costs of raw material and manufacturing costs.
2. The availability of raw material transcends potential supply.
3. Will shipments of logs to Japan continue in view of the situation where the finished product is more costly than if we had made them? (The U.S. is the world's low cost forest products producer). Are trade barriers solely responsible?
4. Russia has great volumes of wood in Siberia which has generally been viewed as inaccessible and mostly undesirable larch. Will a South Korean firm's 1990 joint venture with Russia bring logs from Siberia to South Korea work as planned? The Japanese firm (Tairiku) has had a joint venture in Siberia for a couple of years, but we haven't learned much about their success. Russia has launched a new venture with Finland where the pulp and paper mill will be in Finland, and wood will come from the USSR (Karelia).
5. Will rising stumpage prices cause the use of substitute materials? The price for veneer logs may be escalating to the point where the plywood market place will not support the resulting prices?
6. South American forests (with Eucalyptus etc.) can produce fiber much quicker than we can.
7. What will be the effect of newspaper re-cycling on the paper industry? It is not very costly to convert a pulp and paper plant to using recycled de-inked newspaper, but this could be disaster for remote Canadian plants where transport costs of re-cycled U.S. paper are prohibitive.
8. New paper capacity is coming on line in many parts of the world (generally plant mods rather than new plants). The Union Camp mill in Eastover, S.C. came on-line at 600 tons per day (tpd) in 1984 but was converted to 1,700 tpd. Southern pulping capacity increased from 98,000 tpd in 1976 to 120,000 tpd in 1986 although

pulp mills decreased from 112 to 105. Can the market support this expansion? New plants, meeting environmental requirements, can cost more than one billion dollars. Modifications to increase capacity are cheaper.

9. What will be the effect of 1992 (European case)?. Will U.S. firms go for joint ventures to assure themselves of this market? The U.S. is still the world's largest forest products market, but can this change?

10. Joint ventures in Eastern Europe will entail a considerable political risk and very large amounts of capital. Are their forests to be returned to private ownership? (Imagine the appraisal problems when there are no available comparables.)

11. The Japanese seem to be moving toward an Asian rim market. Will the U.S. be included?

Corporate foresters attend Society of American Foresters and other meetings where they are always on the alert not to engage in price fixing. There is always the possibility that an agent of the Internal Revenue Service or the Department of Justice is there.

The American Tree Farm System is altogether another matter. Tree farms are privately owned timberlands dedicated to the production of timber and other forest products. The program is sponsored by the American Forest Institute, along with county foresters, consulting foresters, and industrial foresters. Timberland owners who are motivated towards contributing to the production sector of our economy become "Tree Farmers", if their timberlands pass an examination. They incur no obligation to sell their standing timber to any firm. Tree Farmers receive publications such as "The Tree Farmer" which keeps them abreast of new developments, both silvicultural and economic. They are invited to demonstrations, field trips, and picnics. There are awards for outstanding work, including annual recognition of the nation's most outstanding Tree Farm, which is quite an attainment when you consider there are about 70,000 Tree Farms. All owners of Tree Farms (usually husband and wife) are Tree Farmers. The system is financially supported by contributions from individuals and forest industry.

In any event, corporations find their earnings from manufacturing are greater than their earnings from growing timber. A few corporations own no timberland at all and procure their wood from the open market as just described. However, the raw material, is so vital that most corporations have traditionally owned about one third of the forest that is needed to supply their mills. This is insurance. When a multi-million dollar plant is shut down for lack of raw material it is economic disaster. There are a few corporations, such as Weyerhaeuser, which own sufficient timberland to be nearly self-sufficient.

Most forest products corporations make their timberlands available for public recreation at no cost. Occasionally, hunting rights to large blocks of timberland are leased to fish and game clubs for nominal sums. Leases may include provisions for construction of hunting camps. The lessor usually assumes liability problems which does alleviate one problem for the corporation. The clubs can also provide some degree of security for the corporation against timber theft and mis-use of the land by vehicles.

The North Maine Woods is an exception. The entire northwest part of the state of Maine, 2.8 million acres, is undeveloped timberland with no public roads at all. In 1948 you could go in a straight line for 75 miles without encountering any sign of civilization. The twenty forest owners use their timberland to grow wood. They have created a non-profit organization to administer the public's use of the lands for recreation. There are 300 developed campsites. Users are required to leave by same peripheral gate that they entered. There are 15 such gates. This ensures that the public will not begin using their private roads for commerce, in which case they would eventually be clamoring for better road service and even governmental ownership of the roads. There are modest fees ($2 to $4 per day or $15 to $30 per season). The lower rates are for Maine residents. Fees are necessary to support campground maintenance. There are tables, privies, shelters, and fire rings. Another aspect are the large logging trucks, heavily loaded with tree-length logs, necessarily have the right of way. Motor homes etc. are not allowed. There is no limit to truck loading for they run all the way to the mill on private roads. They don't need vehicle licenses.

Some corporations supply sporting goods stores with maps of their ownership, and employ wildlife managers. Liability has not been a problem. Should it become so, the policy could change. Vandalism, including damage to week-end parked logging equipment, has been a problem.

The shortage of woods workers has plagued corporations (Irland 1975). The federal Manpower and Development Training Act attempted to remedy the matter, but the program was fraught with problems. For example, government wanted to train the least employable persons while corporations wanted to train available persons with the highest prospects for success. Few of the graduates were working in the field a year after graduation (Irland 1975). A similar Canadian program found that only 29% of their graduates were still in the woods three months after completion of training. There is also the problem that design of newer logging equipment does not permit anyone on equipment other than operators which hampers training. There has been increasing mechanization of logging operations. The corporations are not sure whether it is more economical or not, but it is easier to employ long-term operators of expensive machines when they are well paid.

MECHANIZED LOGGING CAMPS

The Telos logging camp, in western Maine, was a part of Great Northern Paper Company's operation from 1968 until 1991. Georgia Pacific Co. acquired Great Northern in 1991. And, the Telos operation has been moved. However, its 23-year operation portrays a type of logging in remote areas, that are too far distant for contracting with independent loggers. The logging operation was also too far distant for daily travel by their own employees.

Company-employee equipment operators spent three nights a week at camp, working ten- and eleven-hour days. The last day was somewhat shorter to enable safe travel to their homes. Maintenance crews took over for the rest of the week. There were two shifts a day, year around. Much of the work was done with electric lighting, particularly in mid-winter. The camp included 31 equipment operators, three chain-saw men, four mechanics, plus foremen, clerks, and cooks. Hydraulic tree fellers cut down trees with a scissoring action, and then with the same, or different, machine the branches were stripped off and tree-length logs were stacked awaiting the forwarder which dragged as much as a five-cord load to the landing. There it was loaded on trucks. Operators were paid a good wage plus a substantial production bonus. Newer equipment included micro-computer heads which tallied the number, length, and diameter of the logs. This facilitated bonus determination.

HIGH-YIELD FORESTRY

High-yield forestry is based on planting genetically superior trees. Tree planting is dependent on clear cutting the previous stand. It is not feasible to interplant seedlings amongst larger trees. Most would not survive. In 1984, U.S. timberland owners planted 2.5 million acres of trees (about two billion trees), mostly lobllolly pine in the South. More than half of these were on forest industry's lands. Forest industry grows their own seedlings in nursery beds, and even provides seedlings for NIPF and national forests. These nurseries are marvels of efficiency. For example, some produce more than 15 million trees a year with a handful of employees. They can only do this with chemical herbicides which obviate the need of hand weeding. Labor for hand weeding just is not available in the volume that would be needed.

Genetically superior seed for these nurseries is usally produced in tree-seed orchards. Orchards are isolated from stray pollination. Generally when a genetically superior tree is found cuttings are procured from the very top of the tree (the top of the trees produce the most and best seed). Cuttings are then grafted on to ordinary low-growing trees in the orchard. Within a few years the confused tree is producing genetically improved seed, in pine cones, prolifically at heights which can be reached with a stepladder.

High yield forestry implies greatly increased numbers of genetically superior trees per acre which can only be attained by planting. Every piece of ground is used to its fullest capability. Corporations, such as Weyerhaeuser, have been practicing high yield forestry on most all of their lands since the mid 60's. Eventually these trees will support continuance of our useage of wood homes. The effect will be economically noticeable when the first plantings reach sawtimber size.

The IWW and WWI

Many employees in forest products manufacturing are members of labor unions. This is particularly so in the paper industry, where wages are good. Labor unions have been slower in organizing loggers. Possibly loggers are more independent, but much of the reasoning lies in the coincidence of World War I and the International Workers of the World's first big strike.

It was a sad chapter in our history. There have been a number of recent books on the case. Today the descendants of the Wobblies, as IWW members were called, are community leaders.

The International Workers of the World was organized early in the 20th century. Their policies included: leaders could have only one term in office and would receive only token pay; and union dues would be very low. The union adopted a confrontational policy of never negotiating with management. Recent immigrants constituted most of the members. The I.W.W. union activity shifted to the Pacific Northwest forest products industry. A huge strike was slated for early 1917. Strike objectives included attaining an 8-hour day (they had been working 12 hours); elimination of the $5 job fee which laid-off employees had to pay in order to regain their jobs; and improved living and sanitation conditions at logging camps. The strike failed to garner sufficient support and so the IWW carried the strike onto the job by sabotaging production.

The United States entered war against Germany in 1917. Sitka spruce was in dire need for aircraft, but production was seriously lagging. The U.S. Army Corps of Engineers dispatched Colonel Bruce Disque and 25,000 troops to the scene. The troops took over logging and milling operations. By and large they were woods-experienced rural youth. It became known as the Spruce Production Division of the United States Army. Colonel Disque organized a Loyal Legion of Loggers, in effect a company union, and successfully encouraged many of the workers to join with them. Colonel Disque was able to both increase production to record levels and also attain all of the IWW's goals by negotiation with mill owners. Thus it was realized that cooperation can attain objectives that confrontation cannot. "The Loyal Legion was a resounding success" (Rajala 1989). The IWW was villianized, deportations were threatened, there were killings and riots including the Centralia, Washington episode (Tyler, Robert H. REBELS IN THE WOODS). The Loyal Legion continued to function as a union for many years. The I.W.W., however, was considered a subversive organization for decades.

This case history, of the forest products industry, may very well have been the precedent for the more recent cooperative negotiations between organized labor and industry rather than the confrontational approach. The 1930's depression era was marked by confrontation. There were cases such as the Atwater Kent Radio Corporation where the lessons learned in the IWW case were neglected. Kent, from Burlington, Vermont simply closed down his ulta-modern Philadelphia manufacturing plant and retired.

SUMMARY: Forest products corporations are generally responsible land owners with a good land ethic. They pay their share of taxes and require little in the way of services. They provide employment for about 1.2 million American workers. This statistic is dropping, even in the face of rising production, because of increased efficiency, mechanization, and computerized decision making. The forest products industry is free of governmental price supports. Timberlands are not insured against casualty losses from wildfire, storms, diseases, nor insects. Forest industry procures much of their needed wood from NIPF and public forests. Generally forest industry owns sufficient woodlands to provide about one-third of their wood requirements. Forest industry has been quick to adapt to new technological developments. Newer technology will continue to come on line.

LITERATURE CITED

Bourchier, Robert J. Forestry in Canada, Chapt. 8 of *Forests in Demand*, Edited by Charles E. Hewett. 1982. Auburn House Publ. Co.

Callahan, James D. 1948. Crossett — monument to planned forestry. *American Forests*, Vol. 54 (April 1948): 152-154.

Clawson, Marion. 1978. Will there be enough timber? J. For. 76(5): 274-276.

Duerr, William A. (ed.) 1973. *Timber, Problems/Prospects/policies*. Iowa State Univ. Press, Ames. Intro. Page xiv.

Hair, Dwight. 1973. The outlook for timber in the U.S. U.S. Forest Service.

Hair, Dwight. 1978. Does the U.S. face a shortfall of timber? *J. For.* 76(11).

Hair, Dwight. 1980. Timber situation in the U.S. J. For. 78(11).

Hair, Dwight. 1982. An analysis of the timber situation in the U.S. USFS Rpt. 23.

Hayes, John R. 1989. The tree option. *Forbes*, June 26, 1989, p. 268-269.

Haynes, Richard. 1989. An analysis of the timber situation in the United States: 1989 – 2040. Part I and Part II. U.S. Forest Service.

Irland, Lloyd C. 1975. Labor relations in North American forest industry. *J. For.* Vol. 73, No.4; pp 226-227.

Irland, Lloyd C. 1981. Maine's forest outlook. *J. For.* 79(10).

LeMaster, Dennis C. 1978. Timber Supply. *J. For.* 76(6):365-367.

LeMaster, Dennis C. 1977. Mergers among the largest forest products firms, 1959-1970. Washington State University, College of Agriculture Research Center Bulletin 854.

Mayor, Archer H. 1988. *Southern timberman — legacy of William Buchanan*, University of Georgia Press.

McKillop, William, et al. 1981. National impacts of softwood product price increases. *J. For.* 79(12):807-810.

McWilliams, William H. and Richard A. Birdsey. 1986. Midsouth timber statistics. USDA Forest Service Resource Bulletin SO-108.

Rajala, Richard A. 1989. Bill and the Boss, labor protest, technological change and the transformation of the West Coast logging camp, 1890-1930. *J. of Forest History,* Vol. 33, No. 4;168-179.

Skog, Kenneth and Christopher Risbrudt. 1982. Trends in economic scarcity of U.S. timber commodities. Forest Products Lab Resource Bulletin FPL 11, April 1982.

Vaux, H.J. 1973. Timber Resource Prospects. Chapter 8 of *Timber,* edited by William A. Duerr. 1973. Iowa State University Press.

Wiant, Harry V. Jr. 1980. Shifting lumber prices and the silviculturist. *The Consultant (Journal of Consulting Foresters)* 25(3):82.

CHAPTER 8 PUBLIC FORESTS—GOVERNMENT MANAGED

Your chosen spot of timberland has a 27 percent probability of being governmentally-managed public forest much of which is in the west. Typically the probability would be about four percent in the east. Governmental forest acquisition continues with what seems like high acreages, but the overall percent is small. The 1980's were excellent years for governmental acquisition because prices for forest properties were low. Between 1986 and 1989 state governments acquired at least 350,000 acres and the Forest Service acquired at least 50,000 acres. The National Park Service acquired about 2,000 parcels of timberland in the 1980's to protect the Appalachian National Scenic Trail. Most of these were small tracts. Even if government continued forest acqustion at this rate for 100 years it would only shift one percent of our forest from NIPF to public ownership (Armstrong 1991).

THE UNITED STATES FOREST SERVICE OF THE USDA

Establishment of the Forest Service is the story of Gifford Pinchot. He was connected with forests from his birth for he was named after Sanford Gifford who painted the famous landscape "Twighlight on Hunter Mountain" on commission from Pinchot's father (see Chapter 5). At the height of the Great Crusade, Pinchot was a liberal arts student at Yale. When he finished Yale his father suggested he study forestry at Nancy, France. At the time there were a few German foresters in the U.S. No American university had a forestry degree program.

Pinchot completed his studies in France in 1889. Then he advised George Vanderbilt on the management of timberlands that surrounded Vanderbilt's North Carolina estate. Pinchot also assisted in starting the Biltmore School of Forestry on Vanderbilt's timberland. A German forester (Carl Schenk) was the director of the school.

Whereas Gifford Pinchot was the first American to graduate from a forestry school, it should be noted that the Moravian Community in colonial North Carolina had forestry inspectors long before the Revolutionary War (Thorp 1989).

President Cleveland appointed Pinchot to a forestry commission. Pinchot became the Chief Forester in the U.S. Department of Agriculture (USDA). He was in charge of the Division of Forestry, later the Bureau of Forestry. The forest reserves we discussed in Chapt. 5 were still in the Department of the Interior (USDI). It was odd that the nation's forest reserves were in the USDI but the Chief Forester was in USDA.

Pinchot began lobbying congressional friends to have the forest reserves transferred to the USDA. In the interim he concentrated on furnishing free advice and free publications to forest owners. He had a mailing list of several hundred thousand people. Today, one of the functions of the Forest Service continues to be 'State and Private Forestry'. Much of the actual contact with NIPF owners is done by county foresters who are state employees. They do derive some funding and guidance from the Forest Service.

In 1902 Pinchot toured the Russian forests and in his memoirs *(Breaking New Ground)* he wrote rather highly of their forest management. He also visited the Phillipines with a Captain Pershing of the American Army. General 'Black Jack' Pershing later became Chief of the American forces in Europe in World War I.

One of Pinchot's staunchest supporters, in the U.S. Senate, was Vermont's Senator Redfield Procter, Chairman of the Senate Committee on Agriculture and Forestry (the same as Vermont's Senator Leahy chairs in 1992). Note the continual dominance of easterners on this committee. It is sort of an agreement whereby westerners dominate the Senate Committee on the Interior and Insular Affairs. One committee overlooks the USDA and the other overlooks the USDI.

In 1905 Pinchot attained his major goal. The Forest Reserves were transferred to the USDA and the Forest Service was created. There were no eastern national forests at the time. USDI retained mineral rights. Now then, all of this history is meaningful because there have been attempts to transfer national forests back to USDI, or to a new department of natural resources, in most every decade since World War II. The last proposal was in President Carter's administration. There will be more such attempts. They will probably fail. Proponents of such a transfer cite adminstrative efficiency as the dominant reason because the USDI also has great areas of forests. However, the Forest Service and the USDA have staunch supporters of retaining matters as they are. They cite the excellent record of the USDA and the Forest Service as opposed to the continual controversies involving the USDI. In recent years the Forest Service has been engaged in increasing controversey, however.

In the early years the Forest Service was engaged in custodial forest management of our national forests. This entailed protecting national forests from timber theft and from wildfire. Timber sales were minimal until after World War II. The public was in accord with this role. From 1905 until World War II the Forest Service made a concerted effort to attract the very finest available people. The results of a technical examination decided placement on the Civil Service Register. New employees were selected from the first three names on the register. Forest service rangers were adroit in the management of disputes. However, their cooperative nature did not impinge on their forest protection responsibilities. Foresters epitomized public service. In 1914 the Dean of American fiction writers, Hamlin Garland, focused on this aspect in his book *The Forester's Daughter* (discussed in Chapter 5).

Pinchot was not popular in the west for several reasons including the antipathy of Westerners toward expanded governmental ownership. National forests now comprise 39 percent of Idaho's terrain and 27 percent of Oregon's terrain. Pinchot also became embroiled in the dispute between sheep and cattle ranchers. In the current era many environmentalists look upon Pinchot as having been excessively oriented towards wood production rather than amenity values.

Pinchot visited Yale University's School of Forestry in 1905 and began a program of employing forestry students for summer work on national forests. To this day, many national forests requisition forestry schools for summer employees. Schools nominate two students for each described summer job. The forest makes the selection. In autumn the students return to school where many add significant information to classroom instruction. It is an excellent program in that it broadens perspectives of students, and also allows the Forest Service to look over future foresters and encourage certain ones to make a Forest Service career. However, as will be discussed in Chapter 9, there is no assurance that these are the very best that are available.

Pinchot became embroiled in a political controversey. He took a matter involving the USDI directly to Congress without authority of the Secretary of Agriculture. Accordingly he was fired by President Taft and returned to Pennsylvania to become Governor (two non-successive terms).

The Forest Service began to acquire eastern national forests several decades after the withdrawal of the forests reserves from the Public Domain. Proclamation boundaries were established for each national forest, with state approval. Acquisition of lands within the proclamation boundary commenced with donations of forest from wealthy owners along with a program of purchase from private ownerships. Many of these lands had been cleared for pioneer farming and so you can find stone walls, old barbed-wire fences down in the leaf litter, cellar holes, and ancient cemeteries in our eastern national forests. The western national forests were generally never developed as were the eastern. Acquisitions in eastern national forests have proceeded as funds have become available. Many privately-owned in-holdings still await for a willing seller along with a funded buyer. This is evident when you view a large-scale map of an eastern national forest. In some cases, such as the Allegheny National Forest (northwest Pennsylvania), oil rights continue in private ownership which complicates management.

One of the assistant secretaries of the USDA is designated Assistant Secretary for Natural Resources and Forests. This politically appointed person coordinates activity between the Forest Service and Secretary of Agriculture. The Forest Service is a surprisingly autonomous agency as viewed by Congress. The Assistant Secretary does not give much direction to the Chief Forester.

The "Chief" of the Forest Service is usually a career employee who is insulated from the political arena. "By and large, the Forest Service has been extremely fortunate in its chiefs. Fernow, Pinchot, Graves, Greeley, Stuart, Silcox, every one a professionally trained forester" (Schmitz 1940).

The mainstay of Forest Service organization, as created by Gifford Pinchot, was decentralization of decision making. There are nine regions (originally there were ten). The regional forester, who is closer to users of the forest, can make numerous decisions providing they are within established guidelines. The Forest Service is the most decentralized of all federal government agencies.

There are about 154 national forests averaging 622,000 acres. Mergers of national forests, for administration, may change the number at times. The Tongass National Forest in Alaska, with 16.7 million acres of land, is the largest. However, only 24 percent of the total acreage is timberland. More than half the timberland on the Tongass is slated never to be cut. Seven national forests hold a continuous belt along the westside of the Cascades extending from Washington State's Canadian border through Washington and Oregon nearly to the California line, except for the usual highway crossings. They are from north to south: Mt. Baker N.F., Snoqualmie N.F., Gifford Pinchot N.F., Mt Hood N.F., Willamette N.F., Umpqua N.F., and the Rogue River N.F. These westside forests are highly productive.

Each national forest has a forest supervisor, a career employee, who most likely will only remain on that assignment for about three years before moving on to new challenges.

National forests average five ranger districts which constitute the first subset of national forests. The District Ranger is considered a prominent person in the local community. The ranger probably wlll be transferred to new challenges after three or four years. The Ranger administers a large number of employees and an even larger number of temporary employees in the summer season.

The Forest Service also has research responsibility. Eight forest experiment stations (along with numerous sub-stations) are independent of national forest administration. Frequently employees make their full career in either research or national forest administration. And as aforementioned the Forest Service also has their state and private forestry responsibility

National forests are generally managed for multiple uses which include recreation, range for domestic animals, timber production, watershed protection, and providing a habitat for fish and wildlife. Recreation includes both developed campgrounds as well as dispersed recreation such as hiking. Certain rangelands have long-standing leases with ranchers who pay a small fee based on the number of animals, and the annual duration of the grazing allowed, on that pasture. The Forest Service sells standing timber to the highest bidder of specific logging chances. The bid winner has the responsibility of removing the timber within the number of years specified in the contract. Note the Forest Service does not do the logging nor any of the milling. The non-migratory wildlife belong to the state and hence hunting on national forests must be in accord with state fish and game laws.

Most designated wilderness areas, in the lower 48 states, are on national forests. These are single-use, or reserved areas, and are not managed under multiple-use principles. Our wilderness system began in 1924 with 433,000 acres on the Gila National Forest being reserved. The lead editorial in the December 1935 issue of the Journal of Forestry concerned the importance of wilderness areas in providing a wilderness experience for Americans. Included in the editorial was: "Foresters have a duty to withhold desecrating nature's masterpieces."

We now have more than 88.6 million acres of designated and protected wilderness available for public use. Not all of this is on timberland nor forest. About 64 percent of our wilderness is in Alaska, 7 percent in California, and 4 percent in both Idaho and Montana (Zaslowsky 1986).

A few forest reserve lands of the 1890's were designated wildlife and game refuges, such as the Wichita Wildlife Refuge in Oklahoma, which was established in 1905. There are 59,000 acres with long-horn cattle, bison, turkey, and other wildlife. They have more than a million visitors a year in the current era although 45 years ago visitors were rare. The USDI manages more than 400 such refuges with over 90 million acres. President Theodore Roosevelt, a world authority on big game, and who is recognized as one of our Presidents who was a scholar (Burton 1988), was responsible for the original refuges.

Timber sales are the dominant source of revenue for national forests. Administrative requirements for a sale are burdensome and costly.

> the Forest Service has never returned more to the Federal Treasury than it has taken out each year. That is, frankly, incredible! The Forest Service after all, manages national assets which are very conservatively worth $50 billion. ... It is far from being entirely or even very much the fault of the Forest Service (Crowell 1985).

The Forest Service does pay 25 percent of their revenues, and at least 75 cents per acre, to the states for distribution to local governments in accord with the national forest acreage. This is in lieu of local taxes.

Timber is cut in accord with sustained yield principles:

> The continuous production at a high level of the various products of the forest with the objective of achieving at the earliest practical time an approximate balance between net growth and harvest either by annual or somewhat longer periods.

National forests can issue special-use permits, generally for a fee. Non-profit organizations may be exempt from paying the fee. Some special-use permits are issued to corporations which operate skiing facilities on national forests. Revenues derived from special-use permits are substantially more than timber revenues in a few states. Again, 25 percent of the revenues are given to the local communities (through the state) in lieu of property taxes.

The Forest Service has employees who are technicians, temporaries, and professionals. Technicians are likely to remain on the same forest for their full career. They can be hired under local option. Temporaries may be summer employees. They can be employed for many months. They are also hired under local option. Professionals include graduate foresters, civil engineers, landscape designers, archeologists, business administrators, and geologists. Professionals have been employed under the formerly called "Civil Service System".

Before World War II, graduate foresters, desiring placement with the Forest Service underwent a technical examination and then were placed on the Civil Service register in accord with their grade. Vacancies were filled from the top three people on the register. Most states still employ a similar system, including a technical examination. Non-residents are entitled to apply at most all state departments of forestry for by and large they are seeking the best qualified applicants. Wisconsin is an exception, because state law requires employees to be state residents.

President Franklin D Roosevelt was a staunch supporter of the Civil Service system. After World War II a general intelligence test was substituted for the technical examination. In the 1960's it was all re-designated the Office of Personnel Managament (OPM); the register was the OPM register; and all examinations were replaced with an application which was graded. Yes, you read that correctly. However, it doesn't really matter for the Forest Service has seldom hired anyone from the register since President Johnson's administration (1963 1969). Professional hires within the Forest Service now include upgrading of temporary employees, upgrading of technicians, and cooperative internships (Heinrichs 1982), (Sand 1983), (Armstrong 1983). In June 1990 the Forest Service, stung by criticism, legalized what they have been doing for 30 years. They established a demonstration project (which is authorized by OPM) to test a new system for hiring permanent employees. The project encompasses 70 percent of their units, and primarily those which will be hiring. Persons on the registers will no longer be considered in hiring. Few other details were specified, but it appears national forests will employ permanent employees based on some other guidelines which are not specified. These will probably not be the very best available, as was the case in the first four decades of the century.

THE NATIONAL PARK SERVICE OF THE USDI

National parks have an earlier history than our national forests, although the National Park Service (NPS) was established a dozen years after the Forest Service. They have altogether different objectives. The National Park Service is in the USDI. Some states have a park service which should not be confused with the NPS.

Hot Springs National Park in Arkansas was withdrawn from public domain by Congress in 1832. The objective at the time was Congress viewed Hot Springs National Park as a revenue raiser for the federal treasury. The world over, wealthy people were flocking to assorted mineral baths to cure their ills. The matter went largely unnoticed by the public.

Our second national park was withdrawn from the public domain 32 years later during the Civil War. Yosemite Valley had been discovered by a military expedition. This withdrawal from the public domain antagonized very few people for the nation was entangled in war.

At about the same time, debate commenced on the advisability of one more withdrawal. After eight years of debate, and assurances to President Grant that the property was economically worthless, President Grant authorized the withdrawal of Yellowstone National Park in Wyoming.

All three withdrawals preceded the withdrawal of the first forest reserves (later national forests). The first two encountered little opposition. The third had some opposition. All further withdrawals, inlcuding the forest reserves, were to encounter increasing opposition. When John D. Rockefeller attempted to purchase lands around Yellowstone with the intent of giving them to the federal government for addition to Yellowstone National Park he encountered vigorous opposition. He was acquiring these lands under the subterfuge of the Snake River Land Co. He did not succeeed in the transfer until many years later when in 1943 President Franklin D. Roosevelt found a legal loophole which permitted the addition as Jackson Hole National Monument without Congressional approval.

Opposition to expanded governmental ownership of land was, and continues to be, primarily western but by no means exclusively so. An understanding of the viewpoint is far more than the overwhelming ownership of western lands by the federal government. American pioneers, along with many of today's Americans, view private ownership of real estate as developing more responsible citizenry of our Republic. "Democracy" can be used synonomously with "Republic" as long as governments express the will of the electorate. Proponents of expanded governmental ownership of land are usually trying to stave off development in order to protect resources for future generations. There is a difference, however, between ownership of timberland and mere access to governmental timberland which may, or may not be, managed in accord with your concepts. This difference does permeate deeply into the development and character of some people. The authors believe that the United States has an excellent balance between ownership classes, although the pattern is regionally biased. However, there is no way that the regional bias can be corrected.

Yellowstone National Park is a good case history. It was approved by Congress as a withdrawal from public domain and nothing more. There were no funds for protection or management. There followed ten years of vandalism, wildlife poaching, and timber theft (legally known as timber trespass). Then Congress authorized the use of the U.S. Army to provide protection. The U. S. Cavalry and Army Engineers moved in and treated offenders in a rough style which had immediate results. The Army post, Fort Yellowstone is now a tourist attraction. The USDI sent in a supervisor who coordindated activity with the Army. In order to attain funds for essential road construction, and other projects, the supervisor was authorized to grant recreational concessions to businessmen for a fee. This was the beginning of the frequently criticized concession method of doing business on national parks.

The founding of the National Park Service, like the Forest Service, is a story of one man, Horace Albright. The case history illustrates that being in the right place at the right time can be the dominant facet in your career. Certainly Horace Albright was an exceptional man with superb attributes. But, Horace Albright was in the right place at the right time in many instances and he made the right career decisions.

He was a graduate student at the University of California at Berkeley when the professor for whom he was working was called to Washington to be an assistant secretary in the Department of the Interior. After initial hesitation Albright heeded the professor's request and went along. In Washington Albright pursued his law degree, made numerous influential friends, and married the Secretary of Interior's daughter. Later Stephen Mather, a wealthy businessman, became an assistant secretary of the USDI in charge of national parks. Albright worked for him and frequently ran the entire show when Mather was off to one of his frequent trips to a sanatorium. Albright commenced a strong lobbying campaign to persuade Congress to create a national park service. He succeeded in 1916. The dual objectives of the NPS are to make the facilities available to the public and secondly to protect them for future generations. These conflicting objectives mean decision making in the NPS is most challenging. Albright did not become Director until 1929 (Swain 1974).

Horace Albright was Director of NPS during the years that President Franklin D. Roosevelt was in office. On one occasion, while driving through the Civil War battlefields in Virginia with the President, he convinced the President to transfer responsibility for the national battlefield parks to the NPS. Thus the NPS responsibilities today are vastly more than national parks. Included in the NPS in 1992 are

28 national parks
85 national monuments
5 national historical parks
12 national historic sites
10 national memorials
4 national parkways
  National capital parks
  National battlefield parks
  National battlefield sites
  National recreation areas
  National seashores
  Appalachian National Scenic Trail

The NPS never conducts any timber sales nor logging. There is no mineral exploration nor grazing permits. Many NPS employees are seasonal, frequently returning every summer for many years. Historians and nature guides dominate the seasonal hires. Suggested reading include: *Wilderness Defender* by Donald C. Swain; *The National Park Service* by William C. Everhart; and *These American Lands* by Dyan Zaslowsky.

THE BUREAU OF LAND MANAGEMENT OF THE USDI

The Bureau of Land Management (BLM) was established in 1946 by merging the General Land Office (GLO) with the Grazing service. The BLM has responsibility for managing considerably more acreage than the Forest Service, but most of their lands are not forested. They do have some excellent timberlands, particularly in Oregon. Their activities also include timber sales, timber inventories, forest fire suppression, insect and disease protection, recreation management, watershed management, and management of federal grazing lands which include issuing grazing permits. The BLM administers mineral leases to individuals and corporations on its own lands and also national forests.

The value of the Oregon timber sold in 1988 by the BLM was 149 million dollars. The Oregon sales constituted 97 percent of the total 1988 BLM timber sales in eleven states.

Permits for grazing domestic animals on federal lands run with ranch ownership. When ranches are sold the advertisement may include the owned acreage and also acreage under permit. Permit holders must be citizens of the United States. This precludes foreign ownership of many ranches. Nebraska is probably the only state which has laws forbidding foreign ownership of agricultural/forested lands.

The BLM returns 75 percent of their earnings to local government in lieu of taxes. Thus, retention of these lands by the BLM rather than transferring them to the Forest Service (which returns 25 percent) has widespread support. The monies paid to the local community can be very high, and so in some cases funds are returned to the local BLM office, by the community, for forest management.

OTHER USDI AGENCIES MANAGING TIMBERLANDS

There are other agencies in the USDI which manage timberlands. Included are the Bureau of Indian Affairs and the Fish and Wildlife Service.

DEPARTMENT OF DEFENSE TIMBERLANDS

Some military posts include large acreages of timberland. These Department of Defense timberlands are usually managed by civilian employees who are foresters. Recently the Department of Defense has been contracting with established consulting foresters to do some of this forest management.

STATE FORESTS AND PARKS

During the Great Crusade, New York state appointed a commission to study the feasibility of a state forest preserve. A few years later New York state prohibited further sales of state lands in the Adirondacks and started a land re-purchase program. The next year (1894) an amendment was added to the state constitution which stated "All lands in the Adirondack park shall forever be kept as wildlands"

This amendment to the constitution essentially forbade timber cutting, including salvage cutting, on those lands within the Park which are owned by the state. The state owns about 40 percent of the lands within the Park perimeter. Privately owned lands within the perimeter are subject to considerable state regulation, but timber cutting is allowed. The state and private ownership is a patchwork pattern. State-owned lands cannot be considered timberland. A major influence on New York's establishment of the largest of all state-owned wilderness parks was George Perkins Marsh (Terrie 1984: 81).

Neighboring Pennsylvania inaugerated a program of re-purchase of forests in 1897. There are more than 2.5 million acres of timberland in Pennsylania's forest and park system.

Typically timberlands owned by any state would be managed by the department of forests and parks (or comparable organization). Frequently there also are the lands of the fish and game commission, and lands of the various water protection agencies. Most states have formulas to reimburse local communities for the property taxes which are lost as a result of state ownership. Usually these amounts are less than would be derived if the lands were in private ownership. Generally state timberlands are managed similarly to national forests, in that there are timber sales, special-use permits, and multiple-use forest management. State governments do not compete with private enterprise and hence, generally they do not employ logging crews nor do they operate sawmills. There may be exceptions such as programs to rehabilitate correctional-center inmates, but unfortunately such programs are minimal.

In at least one case a NIPF owner sold timberland to the state fish and game commission for a pittance but retained the timbering rights into perpetuity. This means the state pays the usual annual amount to the local community in lieu of property taxes and the owners can continue to log the area forever without paying property taxes.

Some county's, in the Lake States, acquired vast acreages of timberland when owners abandoned cutover lands (Wilson 1932). These are usually managed by the state on behalf of the counties. The counties have been striving to sell this timberland in order to restore it to the the tax rolls.

Table 8 *The Leading Seven States in Timberland Ownership*

Michigan	3,838,000 acres	
Minnesota	3,152,000 acres	
Pennsylvania	2,646,000 acres	
Alaska	2,328,300 acres	
Idaho	861,000 acres	
Oregon	858,000 acres	
New York	711,400 acres	plus the Adirondack Park lands.

An interesting comparison of the Lake States' timberland with Vermont's timberland illustrates much of what we have been discussing.

Table 9. Percent Timberland and Average Growing Stock

	Minnesota	Wisconsin	Michigan	Vermont
	%	%	%	%
Timberland	33	43	53	75
NIPF	40	60	54	81
County/State	40	22	21	6
Softwood Growing Stock	34	26	28	32
	MBF	MBF	MBF	MBF
1983 MBF per acre	1.5	2.4	3.0	3.2

Some municipalities own timberland, frequently with a prime objective of protecting a watershed. These forests may be located in a different town or county in which case the municipality usually pays property taxes the same as any other private owner.

Public-owned, government-managed, forests are found at all levels of American government. People have differing concepts as to how these forests should be managed. We have not engaged in this controversial facet, but have presented background information which is essential to an understanding of these ongoing debates. There are cases where the forest was donated to the municipality or the state, and the donor placed certain restrictions on the land use. And, there are cases where government declined such donations when they realized the donor had ulterior motives which would have impinged on future management. For example, a donor might retain a certain ten acre parcel for enjoyment; and donate the surrounding property along with restrictions on public access, hunting, and even logging operations. And, there have been cases where a donor, in the category of the previous sentence, has tried to force the state to accept by employing political leverage.

SUMMARY: Americans should understand the vast difference between national forests and national parks. One is in the USDA and one is in the USDI. One employs multiple-use forest management which includes selling standing timber (stumpage), issuing grazing permits, allowing mineral exploration, and leasing land to privately owned ski areas. The other does not! It is unfortunate that many writers, editors, and reporters haven't taken the time to learn the score.

If you are flying over northeastern New York State you are probably over the Park. Forty percent of the terrain is state owned. If any logging is going on it is obviously not on the state owned part of the park. There are motels, hotels, and shops but again these are not on state-owned land. If you are flying over Nevada, the terrain below is probably range land or non-commercial forest. There may be cattle grazing but nevertheless it probably is public land, managed by the Bureau of Land Management.

If you are at a public forum, where expanded governmental ownership of forests is being discussed strive to understand both sides of the continuing controversey. It is likely that both are doing what they think is best for future generations of Americans.

Literature Cited

Armstrong, Frank H. 1983. Personal Correspondence with John E. Crowell, Jr., USDA Asst. Secy. for Natural Resources and Environment; Arnold E. Petty, Deputy Director Bureau of Land Management; U.S. Senator Robert Stafford; and U.S. Congressman James Jeffords.

Armstrong, Frank H. 1991. Is government gobbling up too much timberland? Land, a Journal for the Land Specialist, published by the REALTORS Institute. Vol. 43, No. 1

Burton, David H. 1988. *The Learned Presidency.* Fairleigh-Dickinson University Press, Rutherford, Madison, Teaneck.

Crowell, John B., Jr. 1985. Deficits, Compound Interest and the Forest Service. S.J. Hall Lectureship in Industrial Forestry November 21, 1985 University of California, Dept. of Forestry, Berkeley.

Heinrichs, Jay. 1982. The federal job market. J. For. Vol. 80, No.5: 281-284.

Narlock, Rose 1988. USDA News Release. National forests yield $318 million to States.

Pool, Rollo. 1989. Tongass, exploring the myths. OUR LAND Vol.1, No.1 Official publication of Our Land Society.

Robinson, Glen O. 1975. *The Forest Service.* Published for Resources for the Future, Inc. by the Johns Hopkins University Press.

Sand, N. H. (Editor) 1983. Five whole jobs in '82. J. For. Vol. 81, No.1:1

Schmitz, Henry Editor. 1940. Editorial—Why the delay, Mr. Secretary? J. For. Vol. 38, No. 9; 673-674.

Swain, Donald C. *Wilderness Defender, Horace M. Albright & Conservation.* University of Chicago Press.

Taylor, Theodore W. *The Bureau of Indian Affairs.* West View Press.

Terrie, Philip G. *Forever Wild, Environmental aethetics and the Adirondack Forest Preserve.* Temple University Press.

Thorp, Daniel B. 1989. *The Moravian Community in Colonial North Carolina* The University of Tennessee Press.

United States General Accounting Office. 1987. National Forests, Timber Utilization policy needs to be reexamined.

Wilson, F. G. 1932. Wisonsin's County Forest Program. J. For. Vol. 30, No. 2: 155-161.

Zaslowsky, Dyan. 1986. *These American lands, —parks, wilderness, and the public lands.* Henry Holt & Co.

Chapter 9 THE EDUCATION OF FORESTERS

"COLLEGES URGED TO PROVE STUDENT GAINS — WORTHWHILENESS OF THE EDUCATION" This was the headline of a feature article in the Sunday New York Times of January 18, 1987. The article went on to discuss the growing demand for accountability of university education. It related how Colorado is requiring every state college and university to adopt an assessment system, an assessment of senior's mastery of their major fields by outside professional groups.

The writer could very well have added that forestry schools have had such a system for more than fifty years. The Society of American Foresters is recognized by educators as the official accrediting agency. The Society grants accreditation to approved programs leading to a first professional degree in forestry at the bachelor's or master's level. The institution must meet minimum standards for objectives, curriculum, faculty, students, administration, parent institution support, and physical resources and facilities. A team visits the campus for several days meeting with many people. Usually included are the university president, librarian, director of the computer center, forestry faculty, and forestry students. Accreditation approval has been for as long as ten years. In the case of schools which are on probation, accreditation may only be for a year or two. In 1987 there were 45 accredited schools, three of which were on probation. There are schools which have applied but have not been approved.

Students who graduate from a program, which is accredited on the date of their graduation, have numerous advantages over other forestry graduates.

1. They may receive employment priority by prospective employers, especially forest industry and state forestry departments.
2. It is easier to become a registered or licensed forester in those states which have such licensing.
3. Some state laws favor such students. For example Mississippi law stipulates that graduates of accredited forestry schools (at the baccalaureate level) can appraise the value of standing timber and timberland without a real estate license (Armstrong 1988).
4. Members of the Society of American Foresters must be graduates of accredited universities or else applicants must evidence three or more years of substantial forestry related experience.

The accreditation procedure provides the forestry school with considerable leverage in attaining faculty, facilities, and campus recognition. Hence, the process is beneficial to the profession, the graduates, and the forestry schools.

Forestry, the world over, is recognized as a profession. The late Judge Brandeis of the U.S. Supreme Court defined a profession as

> First, an occupation for which the necessary preliminary training is intellectual in character, involving knowledge and to some extent learning, as distinguished from mere skill.

Second, it is an occupation which is pursued largely for others and not merely for oneself.

Third, it is an occupation in which the amount of the financial return is not the accepted measure of success. (J. For. Vol. 53, No.2;145).

The lead editorial in the April 1935 Journal of Forestry concerned the profession. It added that a profession had a collective responsibility of leadership and public service in its own field (Smith 1935).

Forestry schools are located at prominent universities such as Yale, Duke, numerous state universities, Oxford, and Cambridge. One exception was the Biltmore School of Forestry in North Carolina (1898—1913), which was independent of other educational institutions.

The term "professional forester" is redundant. The term "graduate forester" or "forester" implies a professional.

Today the word "profession" can mean an activity by which one earns their livlihood such as professional wrestlers. However, the legislative intent of many laws which refer to "professions" is far more restrictive. Consider:

Tylle v. Zoucha, Nebraska Supreme Court, Case 85-492, Sept. 18, 1987

Issue: Is a real estate broker a professional within the meaning of the professional negligence statute of limitations?

Holding: No. The malpractice statute of limitations applies only to licensed professionals, not licensed occupations. A profession is more than a license to ply one's trade. A profesion is:

a calling requiring specialized knowledge and often long and intensive preparation including instruction in skills and methods as well as in the scientific, historical, or scholarly principles underlying such skills and methods, maintaining by force of organization or concerted opinion high standards of achievement and conduct and committing its members to continued study and to a kind of work which has for its prime purpose the rendering of public service.

Forestry faculty generally have the Ph.D. degree, forestry experience in other regions, experience outside of academia, and are usually inlvolved in research. They are encouraged to take sabbaticals in other countries or regions in order to broaden their perspectives. They are encouraged to provide consulting service, in their field, to governmental agencies, forest industry, and others. One of the facets examined by the accreditation team has been the consulting activity of the faculty, because such actvity is evidence that they are leaders in their field. Faculty are encouraged to publish and also provide good instruction.

Schools of forestry include secretarial staffs who are helpful to students as well as faculty. Forestry techicians provide support for faculty research projects. Many schools have a nearby research forest, and at least one (University of Idaho), has a research tree nursery. Generally there are resident managers on these facilities.

University admission procedures vary. Forestry enrollment has been cyclical with high enrollments seeming to coincide with a conservation era as discussed in Chapter 5. However, it may also be that high enrollments are at times when some prominent person, with a forestry background, becomes a role model for high school graduates. Or, it may well be that high enrollments result from successful youth conservation programs. For example, U.S. forestry school enrollments dropped from roughly 11,000 in 1980 to 4,800 in 1986 (Smith 1987). In 1986-87 accredited schools of forestry granted baccalaureate degrees to 1,278 foresters. Degrees were also granted to 809 master's candidates, and 183 doctoral students (Society Affairs 1987). These are not large numbers.

In 1975 sixteen percent of undergraduates were women and, although not documented, this percentage has steadily increased. Very few forestry students are minorities. The 1975 study showed about 1.3 percent of undergraduates were minorities. This percentage has advanced somewhat since that study. Foreign nationals constituted 3/10ths of one percent of undergraduates in 1975 (Didriksen 1975). This had increased to 3.3 percent in 1984 (Laarman and Durst 1984).

Generally forestry schools assume some responsibility for summer-job placement of undergraduates who desire such experience. These are usually learning experiences rather than woods labor. Remuneration is at the prevailing wage, which is near double the minimum wage. Some students request forest-fire suppression assignments, but such challenges are not for everyone. Summer-seasonal work experience broadens the student's perspectives, enhances their self- confidence, adds depth to later classroom discussions, and can lead to employment after graduation.

Schools also assume a major role in the placement of graduates and in assisting alumni to advance to new challenges years after graduation. About one third of the graduates are employed by forest industry, another third by federal and state agencies, and the remainder by consulting foresters and others such as the military, Peace Corps, and non-forestry employment.

Most forestry schools provide some graduate-level forestry education. Yale, Duke, and Harvard generally provide only graduate education. It is possible for a liberal arts baccalaureate graduate to attain a Master of Science at Yale or Duke in two years. Duke also has a program where students can attain both a baccalaureate arts degree and a master's forestry degree in five years. College graduates in other fields, including liberal arts, have a long successful history of attaining graduate degrees in forestry.

There are schools offering forest technician training. Some are an adjunct of a degree-granting forestry school whereas others are independent.

The Society of American Foresters does not accredit these institutions, but it does grant recognition to programs leading to a two-year associate degree in forest technology. There are about 34 recognized schools in the United States and 5 in Canada. In 1988 there were 481 graduates from U. S. schools and 275 from Canadian schools. This is a continuation of the sharp decline since 1978. About half of the technicians accept employment with forest industry, and the others accept employment with federal or state/provincial government. Average 1987 starting salaries were about $14,500. U.S. graduates were 84 percent male, and in Canada 87 percent were male (Martin 1989).

In 1979 forestry school deans from around the world met at Helsinki to discuss the needs of forestry education. The most important teaching area was considered to be verbal communication. Administrative skills (economics, finance etc.) were considered to be second in importance (Lehto 1979).

THE SOCIETY OF AMERICAN FORESTERS

The Society of American Foresters was established in 1900 by Gifford Pinchot and six other foresters. During the first decade most all members were employed by the Forest Service. Meetings were generally held at Pinchot's home in Washington, D.C. On at least one occasion President Theodore Roosevelt spoke with the assembled group. Mrs. Pinchot continued to host an annual forester's meeting long after Gifford had died. These were baked apple and cider affairs for they never used spirits of any type (Pinchot, Mrs. G. 1952).

In the second decade, the Society standardized instruction at forestry schools. The Journal of Forestry was first published in 1917. By 1920 it was truly a professional society with half the members being employed outside of the Forest Service.

Following World War I the Society became embroiled in controversey. Half the membership ardently supported Gifford Pinchot in his drive to initiate federal regulation of forest management on privately owned forests. The other half of the Society, led by Colonel William Greeley (Chief Forester and former commanding officer of the 20th Engineer Regiment, AEF), were strongly opposed to such regulation. The Greeley forces eventually won.

The third decade (1930's) brought a series of publications, including Forest Cover Types, Forestry Education, and the Forestry Handbook. A code of ethics was adopted and the forestry school accreditation program began.

There are about 20,000 members of the Society today. Headquarters is at Bethesda, Maryland. Officers and staff members testify at congressional hearings. News releases, concerning critical issues, are provided for the press. Continuing education programs are provided. There is an annual general meeting as well as regional and division meetings. Many forestry schools have student chapters of the Society (Somberg 1942).

Thirteen states licensed or registered foresters in 1992 (Alabama, Arkansas, California, Georgia, Maine, Maryland, Michigan, Mississippi, New Hampshire, North Carolina, Oklahoma, South Carolina, and West Virginia). In each of these states a board has authority to make rules and to refuse, revoke or reissue licenses or registrations. Eight can levy fines. Nine can prosecute for malpractice. (Society of American Foresters 1988).

Literature Cited

Armstrong, Frank H. 1987. Do you need a real estate license to appraise and sell timber? Journal of Forestry. Vol 85, No. 7:23-28.

Didriksen, Ralph G. 1975. Enrollment in professional forestry schools. USDA Forest Service letter. USDA Liaison Officer, Box 156, Lincoln University, Jefferson City, Missouri 65101.

Laarman, J. G. and P. B. Durst. 1984. International dimensions at North American forestry schools. Journal of Forestry Vol 82: 620-622.

Lehto, Jaakko. 1979. Forest Education evaluated by forest organizations. Folia Forestalia 398, Helsinki.

Martin, Charles E. II. 1989. Forest technicians: enrollment and employment 1987-88. J. Forestry Vol. 87, No. 6; 19-21.

Pinchot, Mrs. Gifford. Personal conversation in 1952.

Smith, P. Gregory. 1987. Education's changing course (editorial). J. Forestry Vol 85, No. 9; 3.

Smith, Herbert A. 1935. Editorial: Foresters must think. J. Forestry Vol. 33, No. 4; 363-365.

Society Affairs. 1987. SAF conducts forestry enrollment survey. J. Forestry Vol 85, No. 11; 60.

Society of American Foresters. 1955. Definition of a profession. J. Forestry Vol. 53, No. 2: 145.

Society of American Foresters. 1988. SAF conducts registration and licensing survey. J. Forestry Vol. 86, No. 11; 46.

Somberg, Seymour I. 1942. Student chapters. J. Forestry Vol. 40, No. 3; 276

PART IV
THE WORK OF FORESTERS

Most responsible citizens are knowledgeable of the daily chores and challenges of farmers. Foresters are fewer in number than farmers but they are responsible for another third of our total land area. There are about 34,000 active foresters in the United States. Some have no direct responsibility for land management (instructors, researchers, forest products manufacturing plant supervisors, and administrators). Hence the average forester, who does manage land, has responsibility for about 40,000 acres (Duerr 1988). This is 62.5 square miles (or 7.9 miles square). There is daily supervision of innumerable projects along with unforseen emergencies which are usually opportunities to provide assistance to people in dire need. Emergencies range from lost persons to wildfire endangering communities. Forseen daily operations include supervision of logging, tree planting, tree-disease control measures, inventory of the resources, timber stand improvement measures, forest fire prevention and suppression, coping with vandalism, and even eradication of marijuana plantations. There are numerous opportunities to enhance the quality of life for people.

The remainder of this book will be devoted to those facets of forestry operations that civic leaders should know about.

Chapter 10 WILDFIRE IN OUR FORESTS

From 30,000 feet your window seat discloses heavy gray smoke, with intermittent patches of orange, on the westerly slope of a mountain range. There is an army of American firefighters down there although you can't see them. There are both men and women of all races, although Native Americans dominate the scene. The firefighters are tired, hot, dusty, very thirsty, and voraciously hungry. Their monetary remuneration is trivial compared to the sense of satisfaction they derive from saving people, people's homes, wildlife, fish, and immense volumes of standing timber.

The year 1988 was a bad fire year, for wildfire struck about five million acres. The 1988 timber losses were equivalent to 100 billion gallons of petrol (The Economist 1988). Each cord of wood has energy equivalent to 150 to 200 gallons of fuel oil. Hence, the 1988 losses approximated 18 percent of our proven crude oil reserves. On the other hand, five million acres is less than one percent of our 737 million acres of forest. We focus on forest in this chapter because wildfire does not respect the line of delineation between timberland and non-commercial forest.

A few of the firefighters are college students who usually return to college by Labor Day. But September is still the peak of the western fire season. Thus, most firefighters pursue this as a full-time occupation. They derive sufficient income from fire season to sustain their modest style of life. Native Americans, such as the Navajos, have proven to be excellent for this arduous work. There also are permanent employees of the Forest Service, the Bureau of Land Management, the National Park Service, and the various state forestry organizations. If your flight schedule is in a bad fire year there are people from numerous state, and federal, forestry organizations from all parts of the United States involved in suppressing that fire. If you are over California there is high probability that many firefighters are correction center inmates who have volunteered for this type of work, in exchange for residing in conservation camps, for a trivial wage, and for credits against their assigned time. We discussed California Conservation Camps in Chapter 4. If the fire situation is bad the National Guard or Army may be called on to assist, but only after the personnel have received adequate fire training.

There is a fire boss down there. The boss is most likely a forester who has considerable experience in forest fire suppression. There are other foresters who are either in supervisory or staff positions, but overall foresters comprise but a tiny fraction of the total fire force.

The early 1900's practice of recruiting firefighters from a population center ceased with the advent of the CCC and we have never returned to it. Firefighters are volunteers who have undergone physical examination and fire training. The physical fitness examination is the step test where individuals step on to a bench that is 15 ¾ inches high, at the rate of 22.5 times per minute, for five minutes. The bench is 13 inches high for women. Then their pulse rate is analyzed against a chart which includes the individual's weight and age. A low pulse rate is indicative of good physical condition. For example, a track star's pulse rate upon waking in the morning is probably lower than 50.

All firefighters have received instruction in some of the standard courses of formal instruction which are coordinated by the National Wildfire Coordinating Group and the Boise Interagency Fire Center. Successful completion of a course is entered onto their Fire Job Qualification Card. Current fire suppression experience is also entered on the card. All federal government agencies which manage forests, along with the Association of State Foresters, belong to the Coordinating Group. When fires are bad national forests and state forestry departments from distant parts of the nation dispatch trained personnel to the fire. This is one advantage of the standardized testing and training. You may have suppressed forest fires with your town or city fire department. Generally this aspect is not included in our discussion.

Smokejumpers are the elite of firefighters. These professionals are dropped from aircraft and parachute into fires that are otherwise too remote for vehicular access. It is challenging to navigate your drop so as to avoid hanging your parachute in a tall tree. This suppression approach allows firefighters to reach remote fires before they become large fires. There also is helicopter delivery of firefighters to the scene.

Each firefighter carries a three pound fire shelter on their belt. This is similar to a small tent that is fabricated by bonding aluminum to fiberglass. The fire shelter surface reflects 95 percent of the heat, but nevertheless temperatures within the tent can reach 150 degrees. The best fire shelter is the one that never has to be used but most every fire season, in recent years, has included at least one case where firefighters were compelled to deploy shelters. In 1988, there was the Brewer Fire Incident in eastern Montana. Eighteen members of the Wyoming Interagency Hot Shot Crew were cutting a fire line when the fire unexpectedly blew up. The crew moved ahead into a meadow and deployed their fireshelters along an old road in the meadow. The wildfire raced over and around them. One firefighter was critically burned, another had third-degree burns, and two had minor burns but all survived a fire which later investigation reported they could not have outrun. Each of these incidents are investigated to be sure leaders are not unduly exposing their crews in light of the new technology. The crews are treated at a Trauma Center. Most of the lost lives from wildland fire suppression are the result of smoke-aggravated vehicular, aircraft, and roadside worker accidents.

There is practically no possibility that your fire was first reported from a fire tower because technology has replaced most fire-lookout towers. There are about 114 automated lightning detectors in the National Lightning Detections Network (U.S. wide). Automated detectors feed data to computers in Albany, Georgia. Millions of lightning strikes are pinpointed annually. Electric power companies are the largest user of the data, but the Interagency Fire Center also uses the data. Most lightning strikes in the forest do not result in a fire. When lightning strikes a tree the damage can range from a spiralled furrow in the bark of the tree to complete disintegration. Aircraft forest fire detection is important.

High technology is used in all phases of forest fire prevention and suppression. Solar-powered automated weather stations send computers information on wind direction and speed, humidity, wetness of the timber and brush. These facets can change hourly. Computers predict the severity of fire danger. When a fire starts it can be detected by remote sensors, and then computers predict the rate of fire spread, the path of the fire, the intensity, and the height of the flames. Hot shot crews are dispatched by computers, using the assignment algorithm, or linear programming, so as to minimize travel time. Aircraft and helicopters are equipped with "Thermovision" which permits detection of those hot spots that are there amidst the smoke.

Since the beginning of recorded American history forest fires have been frequent and extensive. This has not been the case in Europe. Thus when Walt Disney animated the story of Bambi for American audiences he inserted a great forest fire whereas in the original European story the main threat to Bambi were wildlife poachers. Although not as prevalent as in America, Europe and most all countries are continuously confronted with forest fire problems. This is particularly true during times of internal strife.

The prevalence of American forest fires is, and has been, due to
1. frequency of dry-lightning storms in the west.
2. use of fire by American Indians dating back for centuries.
3. use of fire to wreak vengeance on certain property owners.
4. tendency for some of our tree species to support crown fires.
5. pattern of our upper air current jet streams.
6. tradition of burning debris and other solid waste.

Most forest fires, particularly in the eastern hardwood timber types, are surface fires. They can become hot enough to damage the base of large trees, and they can destroy regeneration. A few fires become ground fires where a fire smolders for days only to break out anew some distance away. The most dangerous type of fire are crown fires where, not only the tree crown's burn but, the fire in the tree crowns may advance ahead of the accompanying surface fire.

Wildfire incurs many costs including the
1. death of people (more than 1500 in Peshtigo, Wisconsin in 1871).
2. death and injury to wildlife and fish.
3. destruction of timber which must be salvaged within six months.
4. destruction of the watershed, and water holding plants such as chapparal in the west, resulting in floods and mudslides.
5. homes are lost thus upping fire insurance rates for everyone.
6. air pollution along with damage to people's health.

In all probability that fire you are viewing was instigated by human action. Incendiarism is the leading cause of American forest fires. This is followed by debris burners and then smokers. The top three causes account for 60 percent of our fires. Lightning causes ten percent of the fires, but this is higher in the Rockies. Other causes include children, railroads, vehicular and other equipment, campfires, and miscellaneous causes. A recent rash of fires, in the arid southwest, coincided with the popularity of the AK-type assault rifles with Chinese ammunition. It seems the Chinese bullets have steel cores that spark on rocks causing fires (Wildfire Newsletter 1989). If you are aware of just how dry the chapparal and other brush in the southwest can become in the summer months you can better visualize the problem. Arsonists are prevalent in most states. In the summer of 1988 it was officially estimated that there were about 200 arsonists igniting fires in California. In Chapter 12 we will discuss the prevalence of marijuana growers on national forests. Some of these people become arsonists in retaliation for their arrest. In 1991 there was an increase in the number of job fires (see Chapter 3). Job fires are arson fires where the arsonists have been firefighters who expected to earn overtime money, or who sought more excitement, or who hoped to receive acclamation for their fire suppression role.

When a person is apprehended for deliberately, or accidentally but in a manner that could have been foreseen, starting a wildfire they will be charged for the cost of suppression along with the value of the lost resources. The Federal Claims Collection Act of 1966 requires the collection of costs. The culprit will receive a "demand for payment letter" from the U.S. Attorney. If necessary payment is encouraged by attaching real estate and personal property of the culprit. Catalytic converters on automobiles do get hot enough to ignite dry grass.

There are three phases of forest fire operations which must be budgeted for in each ranger district.

1. Forest fire prevention includes advertising, displays, lectures, and that prescribed burning which intends to reduce fuel accumulation.
2. Pre-suppression activity includes training, firebreak construction, map-making, computer software development, and detection (aerial and remote sensors etc).
3. Suppression activity includes all activity following the fire report. It is difficult to budget for this phase. Supplemental appropriations are used when necessary to augment the estimates.

Forest-fire fighting (wildland firefighting) hazards and risks are becoming more severe because of the increased involvement of the wildland/urban interface. More homes are being constructed in remote areas. Some of the homes are foolishly constructed with combustible roofing and siding and then they stack firewood along the side of the house. Oregon has a CONFLAGRATION ACT which coordinates activity between the state fire marshall and the Department of Forestry which is part of the Interagency Fire Center. The summer of 1988 the Governor invoked the act on 30 August which caused the fire marshall to mobilize strike teams from counties outside the conflagration area. Strike teams extinguished roadside fires and protected structures, allowing forest fire fighters to concentrate on wildlands.

This wildland/urban interface situation is a problem in many states and countries. There are new questions being asked. For example, if people knowlingly build in hazard areas should they, in effect, be subsidized by the federal government? This would be the case if the Forest Service started training firefighters to cope with building fires. Should new subdivisions in hazard areas be required to have certain ingress and egress? Are mobile home subdivisions a greater fire hazard?

United States and Mexico have an agreement where firefighters may cross the boundary in certain cases, and operations are coordinated.

Fire is purposely used for certain silvicultural operations. Some forest managers purposely burn debris on the forest floor when climatic conditions will mimimize chances of serious tree injury. This is considered hazard reduction. Triggering off a small fire is less damaging than allowing debris to accumulate and then experience a very hot fire. There are other uses for what is known as "prescribed fire" or "controlled burning". These include preparing seedbeds for certain species which cannot root in leaf litter. Certain fungi, which damage young pine trees, can be controlled by a burn which consumes many of the diseased pine needles while the main leader bud is dormant.

Frequently field people, who are directly responsible for these operations, are reluctant to engage in any burning, because if the fire should get out of control, or should the wind change and the smoke occlude a highway, they are directly responsible.

There is a recent school of thought in some forestry circles that wildfire, initiated by lightning, should be allowed to burn in some cases as it would have done centuries ago. This is usually applied to high elevation lands or wilderness areas. Not all foresters subscribe to this philosophy. Our early foresters would not have subscribed to this concept because wildfire was their dominant problem.

LITERATURE CITED

Duerr, William. 1988. Forestry economics as problem solving. p.4-3. The Orange Student Book Store, Syracuse NY 13210.

The Economist. 1988. National parks, live and let die. The Economist Sept. 17, 1988; 34.

Wildfire Strikes Home Newsletter. 1989. Another source of man-caused fires in the wildlands. Vol. 3, No. 1; 8.

Chapter 11 *Forest Management*

People become foresters because they enjoy working in the out-of-doors. They derive pleasure from seeing trees and plants grow. Thriving wildlife and fish populations also contribute to the pleasure of an assignment where each day is pleasantly anticipated. Foresters are proud to be in the production sector of our economy. They are fundamental to the production of lumber and other forest products. Foresters view getting wet, frozen, slapped in the face by branches, stung by yellow jackets, bled by mosquitoes, and annoyed by black flies as just a few more challenges.

Most foresters are involved in forest management. The properties may belong to NIPF, industry, government, or possibly their own families. The first stage in forest management is to understand the objectives of the owner. The objectives are varied, and may preclude the harvesting of timber. Sustained yield forest management is the basis of good forest stewardship. It means the management of a forest property for the continuous production of the desired products, at a high level, with the aim of achieving, at the earliest practical time, an approximate balance between net growth and harvest, either by annual or somewhat longer periods of time.

Many NIPF owners include in their objectives that the forest should pay for ongoing costs of taxes and supervision. Supervision includes marking of land lines along with periodic examination of the property. By and large, it is only selling timber that can bring in revenue. Occasionally there are other revenue producing options such as ski-area leases, maple syrup production, hunting leases, and even the sale of baled pine needles for garden mulch.

It is frequently possible to produce multiple products from a forest. For example, careful harvest of timber can be accompanied by improved wildlife habitat, improved scenic views, and expanded recreational opportunities.

The second stage in forest management, after the goals and policies have been established, is to clearly delineate the forest boundaries and any subdivisions. All states require a survey license for persons engaged in surveying properties for others, and also for persons who record any survey in the land records offices. Usually the laws make exceptions such as governmental employees who survey governmental managed lands, but nevertheless many of these governmental employees have attained a survey license. Unlicensed persons may still survey and map their own properties for managerial purposes but their work cannot be officially recognized. Property owners may maintain their own boundary lines.

Numerous forest properties are considered "land-locked" because they have no guaranteed access to a public road. One recent study showed that thirty percent of a large number of Vermont parcels had no frontage on any road (Turner 1989:35). It is possible that some of these had a guaranteed easement (access) through some other property. However, Vermont and many northeastern states have laws which provide every land owner with a convenient access to remove timber. This is not the case in other states where land-locked owners must negotiate with neigboring property owners for access.

Land survey error of closure for forest properties does not have to be as precise as in urban land survey. Frequently a compass and measuring tape are sufficient. Measuring tapes can sometimes be "chains" (66 feet in length or four rods) for that was probably the style of any earlier surveys. Recent technology has instigated wide use of newer line measurement tools which allow one person to do the work. These new tools consists of a spool of expendable twine (bio-degradable) which is connected to the starting point along with a dial which reports distance. You may encounter lines of string in the forest which indicate the recent prescence of a surveyor. Land lines which are not marked by existing fences, stone walls, or creeks are generally marked by blazing trees, or painting a spot on the trees with boundary marking paint (15 to 20 years durability), or plastic flagging (3 to 5 years durability).

Various forests have differing methods of subdivision organization. National forests are divided into ranger districts and then ranger districts are divided into compartments. Compartments are widely recognized as admininstrative subdivisions of forests. They are geographically identifiable in that their boundaries are usually roads, streams, ridgelines, or other identifiable feature. Logging records are kept by compartment.

Within compartments are many stands of trees. A stand is a group of trees which have similar characteristics such as species or size. Stands can usually be identified on aerial photographs. Unlike compartments, stands are not permanent and boundaries are not clearly identifiable. A "logging chance" is the terrain which is logged under one operation. The word "chance" is quite appropriate.

Forest inventory

The third stage in forest management is usually an inventory of resources. This is the dominant entry-level work of foresters. Formerly this was termed timber cruising. The Forest Service frequently refers to the subject as compartment examination or stand examination. The subject matter as taught in forestry schools may be referred to as forest mensuration or forest biometry. We will use the term "forest inventory".

Stands may be identified in the office from aerial photographs prior to going into the forest. A great deal of the effort devoted to forest inventory is in the travel time to the stands and within the stands. Thus, it is important to glean all of the data so that no one has to return at a later time. This generally means that the inventory should record the location and extent of all resources to include: indicators of wildlife populations such as grouse drumming logs and deer yards; water facilities to include springs; rare and endangered species of plants, birds, and animals; grass varieties in those areas where grazing is important; scenic views; works of man including cellar holes, old cemeteries, stone walls, log landings, old sawmill sites, trails, and various facets about the growing timber.

The objective of timber inventory is to estimate the volume of wood products which could be sawn out of a certain stand of trees by an operator of average efficiency. Products may be measured in board feet, cords, or other units. The volume that may eventually be derived from a stand will vary in accord with the efficiency of both the logger and the miller. Timber inventory is not an exact science. It would be a rare event for two foresters, conducting independent inventories of the same property, to arrive at the same result.

The volume of wood removed in a logging operation will also vary in accord with the type of logging and procurement rules. Chipping of whole trees, at a forest landing, where the chips are to be used for energy wood removes most all of the wood. Sawtimber logging, on the other hand, only removes the main boles of the merchantable trees. A study of a lodgepole pine operation (Foulger and Harris 1973) showed that whereas there was actually 11,547 cubic feet per acre only 6,174 cubic feet were removed when the trees were bucked in a manner so as to only remove material that was 6-inches in diameter or larger.

Usually it is impractical to measure all trees in a stand and so scientific sampling methods are used. There are exceptions such as when trees are large and valuable, in which case all trees are measured. In Europe, where foresters have responsibility for much smaller areas, all trees are usually measured.

Sampling is frequently based on measuring the resources within a fifth-acre circle. A circle with a 53-foot radius enables a person to envision the entire plot from the center. A larger circle might not permit this. The two main types of sampling are random sampling, where the fifth-acre plots are selected in a completely random manner, and systematic sampling, where plots are selected methodically.

The intensity of the sampling (how many plots are required for a specific stand) is calulated based on the variance of the tree sizes. It frequently can be less than five percent of the total area.

The forester's activity, on arriving at a selected fifth-acre plot, varies in accord with objectives of the inventory, size of the timber, and variation in sizes that are found within the stand. Frequently the forester measures diameters and merchantable heights of all potentially merchantable trees above a specified diameter, such as ten inches. Tree diameters are measured at 4½ feet above ground level which is referred to as diameter breast high and abbreviated "d.b.h." Merchantable height of trees are usually measured in logs and half logs. A standard log is 16 feet in length. Results are recorded by species and quality. Defect in a specific tree is taken into account. There is usually no market for dead trees except for energy wood where the trees are chipped and the chips are burned to produce electricity or heat. The recording of data may be on a note pad or a mini-computer for later transfer to a computer where volumes are determined for each tree. In the course of one day's work a forester might well record data for as many as a thousand trees. American foresters have considered employing the metric system, but after an initial trial the matter seems to have been shelved.

The forester also records measurements to classify forest site quality, forest density, and the rate of tree diameter growth. Density of the forest is measured in terms of square footage of "basal area". This means the cross-sectional area of tree trunks at d.b.h. and expressed in square feet per acre. Ideal basal area varies with species and average diameter. Typically it might be 100 or 120 square feet of basal area per acre. Strangely, this is the easiest of all forest measurements to determine. The forester can stand at one point and, using a prism, determine average basal area by simply counting trees which meet certain criteria.

Determination of average board feet per acre, on a specific plot, depends on determining the board foot volume of each tree, summing those on the plot, and multiplying by five to get full acreage estimates. Volume tables are built into computer software and the computer determines the result. A sketch of a volume table follows:

Table 10. *Volume Table, International 1/4-inch rule*
Board Feet per Tree

Diameter	1 Log	1½ Log	2 Log
16"	103	146	183
18"	140	190	240
20"	176	240	305
28"	387	498	636

Trees containing more than a thousand board feet are not common in the east. Value of standing trees is not usually included in timber inventory. However, it might be well to consider that facet at this time. "Stumpage" can mean either volume or value of standing trees. Value depends on species, market, location of the stand, and size and quality of the trees. Price variance has a wide range with certain species such, as black walnut, commanding prices as much as ten fold more than American beech. Typically stumpage values range from $100 to $400 per thousand board feet (m.b.f.). The value of a standing two-log tree with a 20" diameter is $61, when the stumpage value is $200 per m.b.f.

Past rate of tree growth can be determined by extracting a pencil thin core from the tree with an increment borer, and counting the annual growth rings per inch. This is radial growth and so if you find there are eight rings per inch it would mean the tree has grown one inch in diameter in the past four years. Trees stop all perceptible height growth as they reach maturity. Diameter growth will continue, although at a reduced rate.

Inventory usually includes evaluation of the site for producing wood.

FOREST MANAGEMENT AND FOREST INVENTORY

Farmers normally use soil analysis. However, in forestry the problem is that soils which produce excellent farm crops also produce good sawtimber but, on the other hand, there are many sites which will produce excellent sawtimber but are not good for agriculture. Research foresters have attempted to use soil analyses to predict timber site quality but their prediction equations have had low reliability. Scandanavian foresters have had success in using indicator plants. American foresters have had the greatest success in predicting site quality for growing timber by the height of the dominant trees at a certain age. Strangely, the height of dominant trees is fairly independent of stand density. The taller the sampled tree at a specific age, the better the site.

Forest inventories are conducted as the basis for a management plan, timber sales, forest property transfers, managerial accounting, and wood procurement. Inventory is the dominant entry-level work. It frequently is a one-person task and never boring.

The Forest Management Plan

Compilation of a new forest management plan is a relatively rare event. Management plans specify the year that a revision should be conducted. Written plans lend continuity to management. New managers assuming control are guided by existing plans. Typically, a management plan would call for revision every 10 years. Facets of a plan include reporting on unique experiences that have been encountered. This information can be invaluable to new managers. If the plan has been approved by a high official (as is common in Europe) the plan has definite continuity, but possibly at the expense of flexibility. American forest management plans strive for flexibility rather than continuity. European forest management plans stress continuity.

If timber is to be harvested the plan usually specifies the method, location, and time. Flexibility is allowed when time is expressed in a period of three to five years. The manager may need flexibility to cope with variations in market demand. The harvest method can be selection cutting, shelterwood cutting, clear cutting or combinations of these methods. Successful regeneration is frequently dependent on the harvest method. Planting genetically superior seedlings requires clearcutting of the original stand, for one example.

The Timberland Owner's Personal Liability

Laws relating to liability are derived from common law. Interpretation may hinge on the jury's decision, but the following guidelines may help owners. Liability is founded upon:

1. Damage or injury actually happened to the plaintiff.
2. The plaintiffs conducted themselves in a way that did not contribute to their harm.
3. The defendant's act, or omission, was a contributing factor.

4. The defendant's conduct was:
   a. intentional such as shooting a trespasser.
   b. negligent, such as failure to exercise due care.
   c. ultrahazardous which might include blasting or the use of certain chemicals.

The nature, and extent, of landowner's liability is dependent upon the category of the person entering the land.
1. Trespassers are persons who enter without the implied or express consent of the owner. If owners have knowledge of a dangerous condition they have a duty to warn trespassers. Vicious dogs would be a dangerous condition. Implied consent would include the failure of owners to challenge habitual trespassers.
2. Gratuitous licensees are people who enter a property with the owners' permission, but for no benefit of the owner. Owners must warn them of any dangerous condition.
3. Business visitors are employees and people who enter for the mutual benefit of the owner and themselves, with the express or implied consent. These include mail delivery persons, prospective buyers, independent contractors, and fee-paying hunters. Owners have all of the foregoing responsibilities and also must make the premises safe for the visitor.
4. Children, who may not be fully aware of the meaning of "no trespassing" signs, or warning signs, must be protected.

Landowners are responsible for their own acts and acts of employees, independent contractors, agents, and animals. There are rare exceptions such as owners are not responsible for acts of their livestock in free-range law areas. Free range, itself, is very rare.

Liability has not been a major problem for timberland owners. Many NIPF owners find their home-owner's package insurance covers their timberland if it is not used commercially except for occasional timber sales. Otherwise, liability insurance is available at reasonable rates except where commercial activity, such as campground rental is involved.

Property Devaluation From Toxic Waste

Should you spot a few rusty drums on a property you are evaluating as a prospective acquisition it might be well to move on. You also may have incurred a responsibility to report the matter to authorities in a manner where you simply state what you saw and absolutely nothing more. Any implication of toxic waste could result in your being sued by the owner for libel. Environmentally contaminated properties are worth a lot less than clean ones and can even have a negative value. Current property owners of a contaminated property have certain responsibility for the actions of past owners. They could very well have acquired the property at a bargain price due to the contamination.

Summary

The process of identifying ownership objectives, organizing properties, inventorying resources, and composing forest management plans can be very informal. Owners may never have given much thought to their objectives but nevertheless, intuitively they have intentions for their property. The owners may never have heard of compartments or stands, but probably know there is a stand of ash down by the creek or an oak-pine stand along the ridge. Owners may have rudimentary knowledge of their forest resources, or they may have contracted with a consulting forester for a formal inventory. Costs of an inventory might vary from $4 to $8 per acre, but this might be a one-time investment for many owners. They are probably paying $4 to $8 per acre annually in property taxes. It just seems prudent to make a once-in-a-life-time expenditure of a nominal sum so they fully realize the value of their asset. Strangely, few owners do contract with a consulting forester for an inventory or an appraisal. But then, they turn around and eventually sell their timber, or the entire forest, for a bargain price simply because they are not knowledgeable of the current market.

In the next chapter we will focus on foresters who conduct inventories, make forest appraisals, and implement the forest management plan.

Literature Cited

Foulger, A. N. and Johnny Harris. 1973. Lodgepole pine logging. Journal of Forestry, Vol 71, No. 2:93-95.

Turner, Robert John. 1989. Economic relationships between parcel characteristics and price in the market for Vermont forestland. A thesis to the faculty of the Graduate College of the University of Vermont.

Chapter 12 *Extension, County, Consulting and Urban Foresters*

Your state extension forester is with the Cooperative Extension Service at your state university. They coordinate and sponsor short courses of forestry instruction, and general forestry education, for the public. They distribute forestry publications, participate in news-media programs, and co-operate in numerous facets of forestry instruction. If you have a need for a roster of consulting foresters, a listing of your county foresters, or information on some aspect of forestry ranging from taxes to tree diseases, perhaps you should start with your extension forester. You may want to add your name to their mailing list.

There are county foresters in most counties which include substantial forests. They are state employees who encourage good forest management on privately-owned forests. The county forester is knowledgeable of most forest ownerships in their area of responsibility. They provide free service to forest owners who contact them. Sometimes they are referred to as "service foresters." When substantial service is needed county foresters refer the owner to a consulting forester. County foresters coordinate state and federal programs which provide incentive payments to forest owners. They are the first contact to becoming a Tree Farmer.

About 15 percent of the nation's foresters are private self-employed consultants (Gregg 1989). As aforementioned, your extension forester or county forester can provide you with a listing of those in your area. Consulting foresters provide services to all classes of forest owners (Hodges 1989). Consulting forestry is considered a growth sector because only a small number of NIPF owners currently seek their advice, whereas most should. There is a trend for governmental agencies and forest industry to sub-contract out some of the activities they have done for themselves in the past. We have found legislators who are not aware of the existence of consulting foresters. They should know about this facet, for otherwise they must erroneously believe we rely entirely on governmental agencies.

In Chapter 9 we saw that 13 states license or register foresters. The reason is to protect the consumer. In the other states use of the title "forester" has generally not been abused by persons who have not graduated from a forestry school. About 12 percent of consulting foresters are licensed in survey. About two percent of consulting foresters are licensed in real estate. There are about 2,700,000 licensed real estate persons in the United States and only 130 or so are foresters, despite one-third of our country being forested. Fewer than a dozen foresters are state certified general real property appraisers. However, value appraisal of timberlands has been an important facet of consulting forestry in the past. The low percentage of consulting foresters in real estate and real estate appraisal may have to increase because of new federal and state laws (Armstrong 1989). These will be discussed in this chapter.

An Association of Consulting Foresters (ACF) sets high standards for the industry. The ACF sponsors continuing education opportunities;

publishes a quarterly journal (The Consultant); and encourages a high standard of business ethics.

Consulting services covers a wide spectrum of activity ranging from the compilation of forest management plans, and complete management down to tree planting and insect and disease control. The study of forest insects is termed "forest entomology". The study of forest diseases is termed "forest pathology". Consulting foresters enthusiastically anticipate each day's work. Their charges are usually reasonable (Hodges & Cubbage) 1986) which probably reflects the enjoyment of their work.

The trend of the 1990's will be to "unbundle" a great many tasks that were previously accomplished by industrial and governmental employees (Drucker 1989). In the 1980's the Forest Service was subcontracting with consulting foresters for more than $50 million annually. Contracts included tree planting, timber stand improvement, forest inventory, and line marking. Efficiency of the subcontracting approach, coupled with employee-hiring ceilings, will expand "unbundling" in future years. Some governmental research projects are subcontracted with qualified consulting foresters. There also are times when industrial firms and governmental agencies just don't have the required expertise.

Consulting foresters do have associates and employees, particularly seasonal employees. They may be rural youth planting trees on a piecework basis. The basing of pay on the number of seedlings properly planted in the course of a day does provide an incentive which governmental agencies just can't provide.

Foresters are not aggressive salespersons, which is probably one reason why they sought a forestry career. Fortunately, much of their work is referred to them by county foresters who are providing free service and not selling anything. When the county forester suggests, to a NIPF owner, that they contact a consulting forester, the county forester is not selling anything, so there is little hesitation. If the NIPF owner has complained to the county forester about high property taxes, the county forester may suggest using current-use taxation, and suggest a consulting forester. The county forester has no conflict of interest and has nothing to gain, whether or not the NIPF owner enrolls in the program. Whereas, if the consulting forester made the same recommendation the NIPF owner might suspect that the consultant is striving to make a personal gain.

Real estate taxes (property taxes) on forest properties have risen more rapidly than on other classes of real estate since about 1968. Taxing of real estate is a substantial money-raiser for local government. Real estate taxes are relatively simple to administer, although establishment of values for each property is complex. However, this tax does not conform to the benefits received because most of the tax is used for schools, and most forest owners are non residents with no children in the local school. Furthermore, most forest owners have little need for other community services.

Theoretically, real estate taxes are levied on the value of property as determined by what it might sell for in the current market. Standing trees are real estate. Hence, standing trees are taxed annually whereas in agricultural enterprises only the land is taxed. There is no tax on the wheat crop. This form of taxation encourages timberland owners to heavily cut their timber in order to reduce taxes.

In 1817 Connecticut Governor Oliver Wolcott stated "If timber is taxed annually the rates ought to have reference to the remote periods at which income will be received. Otherwise, excess taxation would accelerate the destruction of timber".

Taxing forest properties under full fair market value assessment would mean that if one forest property sold for a much higher economic use, such as a shopping mall, that the one sale would influence a sharp increase in all forest property assessments in that county or town. Obviously there would not be a market for so many shopping malls.

Most forested states have recognized taxing forest properties, where the assessed value is the full fair market value, is basically wrong, and have passed legislation to ameliorate matters. In some cases this legislation is referred to as assessment under current-use, meaning that the sale for a shopping mall would not be considered in any reassesment of property values. Usually current-use tax options are elective and impose financial penalties on owners who elect the reduced taxation and then don't continue with good forest management.

County and consulting foresters maintain continuous contact with independent loggers in their region. They know which loggers are best for a specific logging chance. They encourage loggers to attend short-courses and demonstrations. Logging is a most arduous, and dangerous occupation, but loggers are vital to our economy. Foresters fully understand that we will continue to have loggers only as long as loggers can make sufficient profit to provide their families with an education and other normally accepted American amenities. Foresters also recognize that logging activity should be in accord with an approved forest management plan. Within these constraints a consulting forester maintains loyalty to their client and strives to maximize the financial return.

A case history, which illustrates the work of consulting foresters, is an appraisal of the value of 1200 acres of timberland along with an estimate of the return on investment (R.O.I.), which could be attained therefrom. More important, it illustrates the attorney role.

The case involved appraisal of 1200 acres of timberland in Bridgewater, Vermont. The appraiser included in his contract that he would not reveal the findings and results of the appraisal until such time as he was released from this obligation by having publicly testified in a court of law to such findings. Court testimony has been completed and so the actual appraisal can be discussed. However, I would remind you that most appraisals are not made public in a court of law and in those cases the appraiser retains an obligation of loyalty to the person who engaged him for the appraisal until such time, if ever, as the client duly releases the appraiser from the obligation.

The following information is for instructional purposes only. The authors are simply presenting the case as a non-legal person saw it (Armstrong 1989). The news media should only report on official court transcripts or other legal source.

LOUIS RENE de LESQUEN versus WOODS AND FORESTS BROKERS, N.V.

Louis, a citizen of Normandy, France, responded to a 1981 newspaper ad from a Paris real estate firm regards a parcel of timberland in Vermont The 1200 acres, in Bridgewater, was for sale with a price of $650,000. Louis had a farm, and timberland holdings, in Normandy and could be considered a knowledgeable buyer.

Unbeknownst to Louis, the sellers (Woods and Forests Brokers of Netherlands Antilles) had purchased the property in September 1980 from Harlan Booth for $295,000. The property had been in the Booth family for at least two generations and was reasonably well managed. Booth owned other forest property. He was considered a knowledgeable seller. (Note: only 1.5 percent of Vermont is owned by foreigners.)

Louis, after visiting the property, paid $191,500 down and agreed to pay the balance over a period of four years. The next payment of $134,400 was properly paid in December 1983. The Paris firm assisted Louis in many ways, including making advance arrangements for Louis to export the proper amount of money from France so that he could meet payments as they became due. Such arrangements can be complex in France. The Paris firm never revealed they were making a profit of $34,400 on the sale, and really implied they were working for Louis. The Paris firm gave Louis a written investment analysis assuring him of a 20 percent annual return on his investment. Louis had travelled to Vermont and met with representatives of the seller, and various attorneys, none of whom spoke French. Louis does not speak English

Louis had a timber inventory conducted by a forester, and wanted to start a series of annual selection harvests. However, the deed had never been delivered. (Possibly the sellers were trying to simulate a deed of trust which is not provided for in Vermont law). Louis knew he could not commence harvests until he had the deed. He retained an American attorney who was fluent in French. She was able to get the deed delivered in June of 1983. She suggested that Louis may have paid too much and that the estimated 20 percent return on investment may have been far too optimistic. The attorney contacted the county forester who recommended a forester for the assignment. The forester was retained to appraise the value of the property, and also the estimated return on investment, as of November 1981. The forester agreed to appear in court as an expert witness for an additional fee. The forester found the value to be $291,600 using the market value approach whereby he located five similar properties which had been sold in recent years. The subject property, and each of the five comparables, had a highest and best economic use of timber production. Comparable properties are seldom fully comparable and each must be adjusted to bring comparability better into line. This required an examination of each of the comparables as well as the subject property. The forester worked entirely alone as would be the case in such an assignment. He attained permission from the other owners to examine their properties, because although they were not posted against trespass one must attain permission when the purpose is of a business nature. This assignment was of the most enjoyable type. Hiking through woodlands, recording observations, having lunch with a great-horned owl, simply must be the epitomy of employment. However, the days in court are another matter. Cross examination by an attorney who is striving to make the expert witness appear to be stupid is not enjoyable for the expert witness. Prior counselling with your own attorney, coupled with diligent preparation can ameliorate the hassle. Usually charges for days in court are higher than field-examination days.

Normally there would be no requirement to estimate the return on investment (R.O.I.) but this case hinged on that facet. The forester estimated that the R.O.I., in consideration of the inflated price paid ($650,000), would be less than one percent. Louis had received written assurance of 20 percent. There is nothing illegal with sellers doubling their money in the transaction, but on the other hand, the R.O.I. estimate appeared to be fraud.

In view of the forester's appraisal the attorneys reached an out-of court settlement on some matters, but not all. Essentially it was agreed that Louis would not make further payments beyond the $325,900 he had already paid. That Louis would deed over an undivided fifty percent interest in the property to Woods and Forests Brokers. That Woods and Forests Brokers would strive to sell the property and that Louis would receive the first $300,000 plus half of all above $300,000. Woods and Forests Brokers would pay Louis ten percent of his investment every year until the property sold; and that if the property were not sold by 1990 Louis would own all of the property. During the period there would be no timber harvested.

Louis' attorney, who is fluent in French, was rightfully concerned about the shoddy treatment Louis had received. Hence, Louis was now asking the court for the cash difference between what he had paid to date and the forester's appraisal ($34,300) plus the value of the annual harvests he had foregone due to the delay in delivering the deed and the delay occasioned by the new agreement. He was also asking for three times the $34,300 as punitive damages and the return of the profit made by the Paris real estate firm.

The case was heard by Judge Martin Brody in Augusta, Maine, on Friday May 1, 1987. The forester was the lead-off witness. Judge Brody was hesitant about awarding triple punitive damages but did make the following awards:

$34,400.. the commission for the sale by the Paris firm.

$34,300.. the difference between what he paid and the Forester's appraisal.

$21,063.. the loss from foregoing five annual harvests.

$25,000.. punitive damages.

Judge Brody emphasized that despite the legal practice followed in some countries (which permits an attorney to represent both parties in a real estate transaction) in the case where the realty is in the United States our rules of ethics govern. These include that an attorney, or a real estate broker, can only represent one party and that it must be quite clear to all parties whose loyalty is owed to whom. When dealing with a foreign national, who is not fluent in English, there is a responsibility on the part of the selling broker to arrange for an interpreter to be present at all meetings. The misrepresentation of the return on investment that could be expected was clearly fraud.

Louis's attorney was a superb woman lawyer who possessed the knowledge that was requisite for the case. She readily realized Louis had paid too much; she suspected the estimated 20 percent return on investment was overly optimistic, and probably fraud; and she knew the county forester was the place to start in locating an appraiser. Remember, that initially Louis' complaint was the deed had not been delivered, and nothing more.

The Savings and Loan Bill (H.R. 1278) of the 1st Session of the 101st Congress has changed the nature of real estate appraisals. States have real estate appraisal boards in addition to real estate commissions. In essence, real estate appraisal has been separated from real estate brokerage. State certification is higher standing than state licensing. Certified appraisers are required for realty that exceeds a specified value. Lesser valued properties can be appraised by licensed appraisers.

State-certified real estate appraisers must achieve a passing grade on an examination that is endorsed by the Appraiser Qualification Board of the Appraisal Foundation. Requirements for state-licensed appraisers are the prerogative of the individual states. The significance to foresters is obvious when one considers standing trees are real estate. Some certified appraisers may subcontract with a consulting forester for any timber appraisal.

Business Ethics in Forestry

Capitalism is the economic system which encourages persons to achieve the best that is within them as long as they respect the rights of others. The individual is the prime entity in the United States. In order to achieve perfection the individual must be free. The frontier movement was an expression of the desire of the individual not to be controlled, or interfered with, in their individual pursuits. Capitalism is based on a free competitive market which in turn requires exchange of truthful information. Certain actions may not be illegal by the law, but still violate a professional code of ethics. Courts may rule for the plaintiff in malpractice, or breach of contract cases, where a code of ethics has been violated (Flanagan 1981).

Malpractice suits allow for punitive damages whereas breach-of-contract suits only allow for recovery of losses. "There have been very few malpractice suits brought against foresters... foresters have been sued for breach of contract" (Flanagan 1981).

Foresters, and especially consulting foresters, strive to conduct business dealings in an ethical manner. The Society of American Foresters does have a code of ethics as was discussed in Chapter 9. A code of ethics can have legal standing in a court of law.

Most consulting foresters carry errors and omissions insurance, which provides for legal costs should they be taken to court. This insurance is primarily to cover cases where an unintentional error, such as not including a most appropriate comparable property in an appraisal. It does not cover fraud. Any dubious action is more likely to be considered an error or ommission for an inexperienced forester.

Use of pesticides and herbicides is regarded by law as an ultra-hazardous activity (Irland 1983). Users of these chemicals have responsibility and obligations that go beyond mere compliance with the letter of state and federal laws and regulations.

The following encapsulated case histories illustrate some ethical problems of foresters.

1. A consulting forester, who has just completed a timber sale for a client and received a fee from the client, would not accept any remuneration (inlcuding gifts of personal property) from the timber buyer without the full knowledge of both parties. Even acceptance of a valuable gift with full knowledge of both parties could lead to eventual problems. At the same time the forester must not refuse the gift in a manner which would insinuate the timber buyer was attempting to bribe the forester for more such sales. Judgement would allow acceptance of a calendar from or possibly even a Christmas turkey (but in the latter case the forester might donate the turkey to someone in dire need).

2. A forester, licensed as a real estate broker, would not accept an assignment to procure timberland for Mr. X (whereby the forester is acting as the seller's agent and receiving a commission therefore) and then agree to manage the forest for Mr. X for additional fees. Loyalty can only be totally due one party. One forester-real-estate broker only represents buyers and never accepts fees from the seller. He is a buyer's broker. Thus, this forester can continue to work with the buyer as property manager.

3. A timberland appraiser, who is just completing an appraisal of a property, and then finds the property has been listed and advertised at a significantly lower value, would check his work to be certain there was no error but otherwise the appraiser would not reduce

the estimated value. It is possible the owner had not listed or advertised in the right places.
4. The buyer of a grossly under-priced woodlot would generally be free to conclude matters providing the buyer's knowledge of the market was not significantly greater than the seller's knowledge and where the buyer didn't talk too much whereby any untruths were stated. However, where the buyer is government, or a large corporation, which have many talented resources, and the seller is a low income pensioner with very litte knowledge of the market, it would just not be right. We should hastily add that from our experience good public relations are far more important to large corporations and government than any four- or five-dollar-digit timberland sale.
5. A consulting forester should not contract with a timberland owner to develop a management plan, and then market the timber for a percentage of the price. This forester would have an incentive to cut the timber very heavily which might not be in the interest of the owner. Usually the forester would first develop a management plan, where the timing and the volumes of the harvest were specified, under one contract. Then if the owners were satisfied, the forester could proceed with a percentage contract (Stuart 1975).

Urban Foresters

Foresters are employed in Palm Beach, Atlanta, Philadelphia, and other cities and towns. They are referred to as urban foresters. Their work differs from usual forestry work because they are more concerned with individual trees than with stands of trees.

A profile of urban foresters (Dunn & Gornicki 1978) based on 123 responses showed that 77 percent had attained a BS degree in forestry and an additional 20 percent had graduate degrees in forestry. Their primary work was landscape design, pathology, entomology, horticulture, dendrology, and public speaking. The majority were municipal employees.

Forester in Their Law Enforcement Role

Authorized employees of federal governmental agencies, including the Forest Service, have authority to enforce federal laws that protect public lands and resources. Personnel so authorized have undergone a course of training, possibly at several levels. "Most of the land managed by the Forest Service and the Bureau of Land Management falls under proprietary jurisdiction, by which the state has full authority over the public" (Heinrichs 1982).

The Forest Service has felt that Congress never intended for them to watch over people, but this is undergoing a change for two reasons.
1. State and local police forces are fully occupied in their own domain and are reluctant to range out to government lands.

2. The General Accounting Office (GAO) has argued that crimes in the forest, against people, are doing increasing harm to the resources. And thus the USFS and the BLM should train their employees to cope with people crime. Some examples follow:
    a. Marijuana plantations have appeared in every national forest in the U.S. (Heinrichs 1982). Growers prefer government lands because of the difficulty officials then have in tracing the patches to their source, and also because the lands are not theirs and cannot be confiscated. This production of marijuana is a crime against people, but it is harming the resource as well.
        * Growers use up to 300 pounds of rodent poison per acre which gets into the food chain and kills all wildlife.
        * Growers are using large quantities of fertilizer (nitrogen) which washes into the streams and kills fish.
        * Foresters and loggers shun the vicinity of the plantation because of danger from booby traps. Thus, some areas which should be silviculturally treated are not.
        * Forest recreationists have been beset upon by marijuana growing motorcycle gangs.
        * October 1986: two turkey hunters in Arkansas were badly injured by a booby-trap explosive device.
        * The growers have cut unathorized firewood and timber to build houses and sheds.
        * Rival growers burn each others crops. Some fires spread onto the forest as a whole. For example, 11,860 acres of national forest in Fresno County, California were burned on Sept 14, 1986.
        * In southern states, growers have set national forests on fire to retaliate for raids by law officials.

The Forest Service conducted raids on 3,034 plantations in 156 national forests in 44 states in 1987. They found there were increasing numbers of illicit methamphetamine laboratories on national forests as well as the marijuana problems. The 1987 Forest Service appropriations for drug enforcement were $3.2 million.

The Forest Service also has a major problem with boundary encroachments, some of which have a long history where current owners truly believe they own what they claim to. Many of these owners are hostile to survey crews.

The Forest Service and the Bureau of Land Management have four levels of law enforcement training for their employees. The top level trains under the Treasury Department's Secret Service. These graduates are authorized to carry guns, but not all do. Employees who complete other levels of law enforcement training do not carry firearms. Typical rangers, and assistant rangers, do not carry weapons.

The National Park Service has exclusive jurisdiction, meaning that federal authority supercedes state and local authority. Very few National Park Sevice employees are authorized to carry weapons. The matter is complex. For example, parts of the Appalachian Trail are on national forests, state forests, and national parks. But nearly half of the trail is on land that was recently acquired from NIPF and forest industry by the NPS and is being administered by the Appalachian Trail Conference and member clubs. Police work on these parts of the trail are being negotiated between the member clubs and local authorities because Congress has not authorized funds for the NPS to police these lands. Violent crime along the trail does occur.

All classes of forest ownership experience problems including: boundary encroachments, timber trespass (legal terminology for stealing standing timber), property thefts, vandalism, arson fires, damage to woods roads, and firewood thefts. Vandalism to logging equipment has been particularly bad. Forest owners can take preventive measures which are very successful in some cases.

1. Maintain excellent relations with the local people and especially their teenagers. Don't unecessarily post against trespass. Visit and socialize. Whereas you may not pick up hitchhikers normally there can be exceptions when you encounter a local farm youth walking home. And hire local youth when you have a need for a helping hand.
2. Know your neighboring property owners; send them a map of your property; inform them how your boundaries are marked; advise them in advance of logging operations; inform them of your long-range plans; and advise them of any unusual developments or facets of their ownership. However, don't incur any liability such as telling them someone has crossed over their line in a logging operation when you are not a licensed surveyor who is qualified to make that judgement.
3. Tour your land lines periodically and keep them well identified.
4. Safeguard personal property by removing it when possible, or by marking it with a number or mark you can positively identify the property by. There are organizations which coordinate such property marking. Usually they also label items with decals to warn thieves.

Forestry Research

There is ongoing forestry research by many organizations. Persons who make careers in forestry research usually have graduate degrees.

The Forest Service's forest experiment stations were discussed in Chapter 8. There are eight main stations plus numerous regional stations which are frequently located on state universities' lands. Sometimes the staff are adjunct professors at the university and teach courses. The main stations have mailing lists where they periodically inform people of the available publications. There is also the Forest Products Laboratory at Madison, Wisconsin which has a long successful record of the most meaningful accomplishments. Addresses are listed in the appendix.

State forestry organizations do research that is needed, and is not being done by the Forest Service or elsewhere. Sometimes states subcontract research to a consulting forester.

Forest products corporations do necessary research to fill in gaps in essential information that is not being done by governmental agencies. Some corporations maintain a sizeable research staff.

Forestry school faculty members perform research as discussed in Chapter 9, and even some NIPF owners do meaningful research.

Foresters and Politics
(Published in the Journal of Consulting Foresters Vol. 25, No. 1,1980)
(Excerpts from the paper by Frank H. Armstrong)

Two notable eras of progress for American forestry were when foresters engaged in our nation's main political arena. Forester Gifford Pinchot was a confidant, consultant and friend to President Theodore Roosevelt. American forestry made great strides in this era. As early as 1928, President Franklin D. Roosevelt spoke of himself as a forester although he graduated from Columbia University Law School and was not a graduate forester. He became an associate member of the Society of American Foresters while he was Governor of New York, and he was the first recipient of the Society's Sir William Schlich Memorial Medal. American forestry made good progress while Franklin D. Roosevelt was President.

Four foresters have been Governors — Gifford Pinchot of Pennsylvania, Sherman Adams of New Hampshire, and B. F. Heintzleman was Territorial Governor of Alaska prior to statehood. There was the aforementioned governorship of Franklin D. Roosevelt. In all four cases state forestry made excellent progress in the years that a forester was governor.

One forester ran for Lieutenant Governor of Virginia a few years past and although he did not win, he made a very credible showing. There have been foresters in Congress such as Bill Meyer of Vermont. There have been no foresters in Congress for the last two decades. However, there have been (and there are) foresters who are congressional staff members. Forester membership in professional organizations and associations is often high. These organizations are effective political voices.

Foresters are well suited to engage in politics. They are members of a profession that strives to use forests to enhance the quality of life; they are concerned with helping other people; their goals are on a higher plane than the maximization of personal income; they have an excellent work ethic; and they have a well-rounded intellectual education. Foresters are professionals and accordingly are far more than competent technicians. Some foresters cannot engage in political activity by terms of their employment.

All fifty states have a state senate with a grand total of 1,967 seats. In

1980 there was one forester in the state senate of Montana, New Hampshire and North Carolina. Forty-nine states have a house of representatives (Nebraska being the lone exception). The national grand total in 1980 was 5,593 seats in the various houses. There was one forester in the state house of representatives in Florida, Georgia, Montana, New Hampshire, Oregon, Washington and West Virginia. This works out to there having been one forester in state legislatures for every 756 members. There are 3,070 counties in the United States, most of them having a county chairman for each of the major political parties and, of course, there is a state chairman in each state. Virginia had two county chairmen in the late 1970's. In 1980 there were two county chairmen in New Hampshire and one in Vermont. In the compilation of the above data from associates in each state, in 1980, the author received the following comments.

From Arizona: "The recently appointed and confirmed State Land Commissioner who is also the State Forester by law is a graduate Forester for the first time since Statehood in 1912. He appoints a deputy State Forester who also by law is required to be a graduate forester.

Perhaps one of the reasons for the good image and reputation of foresters in the pre-Monogahela period of American Forestry was the fact that Society perceived the Forester as not having a vested interest. The need to satisfy Society's ever-increasing demands for Forest Products has recently put the forester into a position of appearing "pro-industry" rather than "pro-environment" and thus, appearing to now have a vested interest.

This is unfortunate, and perhaps becoming more politically active is the road to reversing the current perceptions of the Post-Materialists as Ron Arnold calls them.

"The State of Alaska has one forester who is a borough (county) assemblyman. The State Forester was in the State House of Representatives prior to his re-election loss."

From Florida: "Foresters should become more involved in the political arena. The SAF has not been structured to encourage this. The proposed organization of Sections by states should get more foresters to thinking about politics. This is long overdue."

From Indiana: "No foresters in the state legislature now. Senator defeated in last primary."

From Virginia: "Foresters have not been noted for their legislative activities even though they are supportive of many legislative programs nationally, and in their own states they have not taken part in the political processes that lead to their election."

"Numbers of foresters in New Hampshire are involved locally as selectmen, school boards, planning boards etc."

From Montana: "Regards foresters in the legislature both are members of Western States Legislative Forestry Task Force (2 senators, 2 representatives from each state of Alaska, California, Idaho, Oregon, Washington, Montana)."

From South Carolina: "Checked biographics of U.S. Senators and Congressmen, couldn't spot any indicating they were graduate foresters. I understand a University of Georgia forestry graduate served as a member of the Georgia House of Representatives. Don't know if he was re-elected..."

"In North Carolina foresters don't often participate in politics by actively seeking elected political office."

"Your letter regarding political activities of foresters raises many interesting points. In Kentucky, most of the foresters are either federal or state employees, and thus are barred by the Hatch Act and the State Merit System from engaging in partisan political activities."

This 1980 study revealed that few foresters enter the political arena. Some cannot do so by nature of their employment. Others prefer to avoid such highly competitive challenges. Forester "Bill" Meyer was elected to one term in Congress from Vermont in the 1960's. Perhaps his experience is evidence of problems which foresters have in satisfying voters. Foresters, by nature of their education, have a long-term view of most every situation. They are generally more concerned about future generations than they are about the present generation of average voters. This may be very well, but it just doesn't sell in today's political arena.

Summary

Civic leaders and future civic leaders, particularly of the heavily forested states, can be far more effective knowing the facets we have discussed in this text. We have treated some matters rather lightly but this was done with deliberation. Lawyers should recognize cases where people have been defrauded and they should know where to go to contract with the proper expert witness for that particular case. Bankers should not be surprised when a low-income family expresses a request for financing of timberland. Legislators should be wary of their colleagues who suggest increasing taxes on timberland owners, espcecially when they justify their program by the trite "after all, they are nearly all very rich people". Members of the clergy should understand that physically challenging forestry work, especially on family-owned timberland, may be the best prescription for some wayward youth.

Literature Cited

Armstrong, Frank H. 1980. Foresters and politics. Journal of Consulting Foresters, Vol. 25, No. 1.

Armstrong, Frank H. 1989. Non-residential real estate appraisal and essentials of real estate. Correspondence Course offered by Dept. of Forestry, Univ of Vermont, Burlington, VT 05405.

Armstrong, Frank H. and Robert G. Willhite. 1989. Law on Real Estate Appraisal. Journal of Forestry Vol. 87, No. 12.

Drucker, Peter. 1989. Peter Drucker's 1990s. The Economist Vol. 313, No. 7625: 19-24.

Dunn, B. Allen & Philip P. Gornicki. 1978. Professional profile of urban foresters practicing in the eastern United States. Journal of Forestry Vol. 76, No. 4; 215-216.

Flanagan, David T. 1981. Legal considerations of professional ethics. Journal of the Assn. of Consulting Foresters, Vol. 26, No. 3:59-64.

Gregg, N. Taylor, Editor. 1989. Forestry Employment Outlook. Jour. of Forestry Vol. 87, No. 11:53.

Heinrichs, Jay. 1982. Cops in the woods. Journal of Forestry Vol. 80, No.11; 722-725.

Hodges, Donald G. 1989. The roles of forestry consultants; their importance and changing responsibilities. Journal of the Assn of Consulting Foresters Vol 34, No. 3.

Hodges, Donald G. and Frederick W. Cubbage. 1986. A comparison of forestry consultant surveys. The Jour. of the Assn. of Consulting Foresters, Vol. 31, No. 3:64-68.

Irland, Lloyd. C. 1983. Pesticides: Ethical problems for foresters. Journal of the Assn. of Consulting Foresters, Vol. 28, No. 1:17-20.

Stuart, Edward, Jr. A.C.F. 1975. Professional ethics and the A.C.F. J. of Consulting Foresters, Vol 20, No. 2: 32-35.

Appendix A to Window Seat

COMMONLY USED UNITS OF MEASUREMENT IN FORESTRY, FORESTRY FACTS
UNITS OF DISTANCE:
1 rod (pole) = 16.5 feet
1 chain = 66 feet or 4 rods or 22 yards or 20.1168 meters
1 mile = 80 chain or 5280 feet or 1760 yards

UNITS OF AREA:
1 acre = 43,560 sq. ft. or 10 square chains or 208.7 ft. x 208.7 ft.
1/5th acre = circle with a radius of 52.7 ft.
1 section = 1 square mile or 640 acres = 2.59 Sq. Kilometers.
1 township = 36 sections or 6 miles by 6 miles
First Division Grant (parts of New England) 160 rods by 105 rods or 2640 ft. by 1732.5 ft. or 40 chains by 26.25 chains or 1/2 mile by 0.328 mile or 105 acres
1 hectare = 2.5 acres

UNITS OF VOLUME:
1 board foot (bf) = 12 cubic inches or 1 ft. by 1 ft. by 1 inch.
1,000 board feet = 1 mbf
1 cord = 4 ft. by 4 ft. by 8 ft. or 128 cubic feet of wood, bark, and air.
1 cubic meter = 35.3147 cubic feet
1 cubic ft. = 0.028 cu. meters
1000 cubic feet = 1 cunit

APPROXIMATE EQUIVALENTS:
1 cord = 128 cu. ft. of wood, air, and bark or 85 cubic feet solid wood.
For 12" diam. (small end) logs 1 mbf = 138.5 cu. ft. or 1.6 cords
" " " 1 cu. ft. = 7.22 board feet
(1 cord = 0.625 mbf)
For 18" diam (small end) logs 1 mbf = 123 cu. ft. or 1.5 cords
" " " 1 cu. ft. = 8.13 board feet
(1 cord = 0.67 mbf)

METRIC EQUIVALENTS:
One cord = 85 Cu. Ft. = 2.41 cubic meters
One cubic foot = 0.28 cubic meters

OTHER FOREST MEASUREMENTS:
D.B.H. or d.b.h. = tree diameter at breast high (4.5 ft. above ground)
d.i.b. = diameter inside bark (usually at the small end of log)
1 log = 16 foot section of tree trunk
Form Class (measure of tree taper) = d.i.b./d.b.h. where d.i.b. is at the top of the first log.

APPENDIX A

OTHER USEFUL FACTS:
Total land area in the United States is 2.3 billion acres.
(32% forest; 25% pasture-range; 20% cropland; 15% tundra, swamp, desert and water; 8% urban, highways, and parks).
(Superimposed on the forest, range, tundra etc. are 90.8 million acres of designated wilderness areas (4% of the total land area).
The Federal Government owns 762 million acres of land (all classes) Bureau of Land Management (USDI) controls 470 million acres. U.S. Forest Service (USDA) controls 190 million acres. National Park Service (USDI) controls 70 million acres. U.S. Fish and Wildlife Service (USDI) cntrls 33.9 million acres.
Alaska is 96.4% federally owned.
Nevada is 86.6% federally owned
Utah is 66% federally owned.
Idaho is is 64% federally owned.
States, counties, and municipalities own 138 million acres.
Land held in trust for Native Americans is 46 million acres.
Land privately owned is 1.3 billion acres.
One-third of the U.S. is covered by wooded areas (forest)
(737 million acres)
Timberland is the wooded area capable of growing 20 cubic feet of wood per acre annually and not reserved legally from timber production. There are 482 million acres of timberland.
The productive forest base, on which repeated crops of trees are being grown for commerce, is about 260 million acres (about one acre per person).
1.9 billion trees are being planted annually in the mid-1980's. That's 8 trees per person. Forest industry accounts for 55 percent, NIPF account for 28 percent, and government accounts for 17 percent. The leading states (in order) are Georgia, Florida, Alabama, Mississippi, Oregon, and Washington.
Ownership of timberland: 60 percent by farm and family known as non-industrial private forests, 13 percent by forest industry, and 27 percent by government.
Net annual growth of sawtimber is 21 percent greater than removals plus mortality.
National forests provide about 22 percent of the total wood volume consumed annually (In 1987 12.7 million mbf, an all-time record for national forests).
WILDERNESS AREAS: Congress has designated 474 wilderness areas totaling 90.8 million acres (4% of the U.S.A.). Locations include 57.2 million are in Alaska; 5.9 million in California; 3.9 million in Idaho; 3.4 million in Montana; 3 million in Wyoming; 2.5 million in Washington; 2.1 million in Oregon; and 1.5 million in New Mexico)

The only states without federal wilderness areas are Connecticut, Rhode Island, Delaware, Maryland, Kansasa, and Iowa.

The millions of wilderness acres managed by federal agencies include: National Park Service—38.5 percent; Forest Service—32.5 percent; Fish & Wildlife Service 19.3 percent; and Bureau of Land Management 0.5 percent.

PAPER FACTS:

U.S. consumption of newsprint has been rising at 4 to 5 percent annually in recent years. It was 12,336,000 tons in 1988 (about 4.5 million tons of newspaper were recycled. Fifty-three percent came from Canada in the late 1980's, but is dropping in the early 1990's due to the economy and U.S. recycling.

Canada exported 597,000 metric tons of newsprint to the U.S. in the month of November 1987. This was 75 percent of their production.

The Forest Service estimates domestic demand for paper will more than double between 1988 and 2030. In 1987 our per capita consumption of paper was a little more than 600 pounds.

The Sunday New York Times uses the equivalent of about 75,000 trees (8 inches dbh) per each issue.

CHRISTMAS TREES:

Americans buy about 30 million Christmas trees every year.

RECREATION:

Snowmobiles: 23,000 registered in Vermont in 1987. 160 clubs with 16,000 members coordinated by Vermont Assoc. of Snow Travellers. There are about 3,500 miles of snow trail in Vermont.

FOREST INDUSTRY EMPLOYEES:

In 1987 there were about 1,256,000 employees in forest industry. There were 643,100 in logging and lumber and solid wood products production, with average annual earnings of $16,100. There were 612,900 persons in paper manufacturing with average annual earnings of $24,300.

In 1992, in response to the economic recession, along with further automation, employees in forest industry have dropped to about one million.

TREE MORTALITY:

It is not unusual for forests to start with 15,000 seedlings per acre and end up 60 years later with 100 big trees. The others die because of competition, or are salvaged by thinning operations.

TRANSPIRATION:

An acre of well-stocked maple trees can give off 8,000 gallons of water through evaporation in a single growing season.

APPENDIX A

ENERGY FACTS:
- 1 cord of wood is equivalent to 150 to 200 gallons of fuel oil.
- 1 mbf (large wood) is equivalent to 225 to 300 gallons of fuel oil.
- 1 mbf (small wood) is equivalent to 240 to 320 gallons of fuel oil.
- 120 pounds of air-dried hardwood = 8 gallons motor gasoline = 1 million BTU
- 60 million tons of air-dried hardwood = 171 million barrells crude oil = 1 quadrillion BTU   (QUAD)
- U.S. Consumption in 1987 = 77 Quads
- U.S. Production in 1987 = 65 quads
- U.S. Crude oil Prod. 1987 = 18 quads.
- U.S. proven crude oil reserves = 27 billion barrells
  (NOTE 1 barrell crude = 42 gallons, but produces only about 22 gallons of gasoline/petrol).

APPENDIX B:
THE REFORESTATION INCOME TAX INCENTIVE, EXAMPLE
(Continuation of Chapter 5)

Consider a married couple who own 100 acres of forest under "Tenancy by the Entirety" (the usual method). They have two children. Their 1988 joint taxable income was $30,000. Hence their 1988 income tax was $4,532.50. They are in the 28 percent federal income tax bracket. There also were state income taxes. Assume the state income tax was pegged to the federal income tax at 24 percent. State taxes can be itemized on the federal income tax return so by an iterative procedure it can be determined that they were in the 32.5 percent state and federal income tax bracket.

They invested $1,000 in reforestation in 1988, 1989, and 1990 and no more:

AMORTIZATION ($)
(Adjustments to income)

YEAR	1988	1989	1990	TOTAL	TAX SAVING/CREDIT	TAX SAVING	TOTAL
1988	71.43			71.43	23.21	100	123.21
1989	142.86	71.43		214.29	69.64	100	169.64
1990	142.86	142.86	71.43	357.15	116.07	100	216.07
1991	142.86	142.86	142.86	428.58	139.29		139.29
1992	142.86	142.86	142.86	428.58	139.29		139.29
1993	142.86	142.86	142.86	428.58	139.29		139.29
1994	142.86	142.86	142.86	428.58	139.29		139.29
1995	71.43	142.86	142.86	357.15	116.07		116.07
1996		71.43	142.86	214.29	69.64		69.64
1997			71.43	71.43	23.21		23.21

TOTAL DOLLARS RECOVERED FROM $3,000 $1,275.00

In this case the owners recovered $1,275.00 from their $3,000 investment and so their actual costs were $1,725. However, money does have time value. If we assumed the owners invested each annual return (tax saving) at 6 percent compound interest, and that their opportunity costs of the three 1000-dollar investments was 6 percent, their actual costs as of 1988 were $1,852.51 (the discounted cost in 1988 at 6%). This assumes the expenditures were made near the beginning of the year and that each tax saving was received at the end of the year.

$-1,000(1.06)^{10} - 1,000(1.06)^9 - 1,000(1.06)^8 + 123.21(1.06)^9 +$

$169.64(1.06)^8 + 216.07(1.06)^7 + 139.29(1.06)^6 + 139.29(1.06)^5 +$

$139.29(1.06)^4 + 139.29(1.06)^3 + 116.07(1.06)^2 + 69.64(1.06) +$

23.32 = value in 1997.

and $\dfrac{-3,317.56}{1.06^{10}} = -1,852,51$ (the discounted cost in 1988 at 6%)

APPENDIX C: *Addresses and Glossary of Forestry Related Terms*

ADDRESSES:
  Society of American Foresters, 5400 Grosvenor Lane, Bethesda, MD 20814 Tel 301 897 8720
  American Forestry Assn. P.O. Box 2000, Washington, D.C. 20013
  American Forest Council (Tree farm system) 1250 Connecticut Ave. NW Suite 320, Washington DC 20036 (202 463 2455)
  Association of Consulting Foresters, 5410 Grosvenor Lane, Suite 205, Bethesda, MD 20814
  National Arbor Day Foundation Suite 501, 211 North 12th, Lincoln, Nebraska, 68508 (402 474 5655)
  American Pulpwood Assn., 1025 Vermont Ave NW, Suite 1020, Washington DC 20005
  Bureau of Land Management, USDI, Washington DC 20240
  Extension Service, U.S. Dept. of Agriculture, Washington DC 20250
  Fish and Wildlife Service, USDI, Washington DC 20240
  Forest Service, USDA PO box 96090, Washington DC 20090-6090
  International Right of Way Assn., 9920 LaCienega Blvd., Suite 515, Inglewood, CA 90301
  National Forest Products Assn., 1250 Connecticut Ave, NW, Washington DC 20036
  National Park Service, USDI, PO Box 37127, Washington DC 20013-7127
  Vermont Assoc. of Snow Travelrs (VAST) 156 Main St., Box 839, Montpelier, Vermont 05602 (802) 229 0005

GLOSSARY OF FORESTRY RELATED TERMS:

AFFORESTATION = establishment of a forest on an area not previously forested or which has not been forested for a long time.

AIR DRY = lumber or other wood products that have been dried by exposure to atmospheric conditions so the water content is in equilibrium with the surrounding atmosphere.

ALLOWABLE CUT = the amount of wood that can be harvested annually or periodically in acccord with management objectives such as sustained yield.

ASPECT = the compass direction towards which a slope faces.

AREA REGULATION = a method of controlling timber harvest by acreage that is annually or periodically cut.

BACK CUT = the final cut in tree felling.

BACKFIRE = a fire deliberately set in front of an advancing forest fire in an effort to check the wildfire by removing the fuel supply.

BARE-ROOT SEEDLING = a tree seedling grown in a nursery bed and then lifted and the roots kept moist until it can be planted.

BASAL AREA = the cross-sectional area of tree trunks at breast high (4½ ft.) and expressed in square feet. It is a measure of stand density.

BERM = the outside or downhill side of the shoulder of a road.

BILTMORE STICK = a ruler-like stick used in estimating height and diameter of trees.

BLOWDOWN = a stand of timber which has been blown down by the wind.

BLUESTAIN FUNGUS = a common form of fungal stain that develops in dead trees, logs, and green lumber which reduces the grade of the wood but not the strength. It can be avoided by rapid processing of trees to produce dry lumber.

BOARD FOOT = a standard unit of timber measure equal to a board one foot long, one foot wide, and one inch thick.

BOLE = a tree trunk that is large enough to produce saw timber.

BOLT = a short log (8 ft or less) used for pulpwood or veneer.

BOREAL = northern.

BROWSE = buds, shoots, and leaves of woody plants eaten by wildlife or domestic animals.

BUFFER STRIP = a corridor of vegetation that is left between a road or stream and a timber harvest area.

BUTT ROT = wood decay or rot at the base of a tree.

CAMBIUM LAYER = the cells between the sapwood and the inner bark of a tree. Each growing season the cambium (by cell division) produces a new layer on each side.

CANOPY = the continuous cover of branches and foliage over a stand of trees.

CANT = a log that is square cut by slabbing the four sides.

CAT FACE = a scar caused by fire or logging damage to the trunk of a tree.
CELLULOSE = a complex carbohydrate occuring in the secondary cells of wood and other vegetable material.
CHAIN = a measure of length used in land surveying. It is 66 feet.
CHANCE (LOGGING CHANCE) = the terrain encompassed by a logging operation.
CHECK = a crack in lumber, a log, or a tree.
Chip-N-Saw = the registered trade name for a machine that makes small logs into cants by chipping out the slabs.
CHOKER = a self-tightening noose of wire cable in logging.
CLEARCUTTING = the harvest of an entire stand of trees, although some unsaleable material may be left.
CLIMAX FOREST = the culminating stage of natural succession of a forest community. Thereafter, barring any setback, it will maintain itself with the same species mix.
CLONE = genetically identical plant material.
CO-DOMINANT = One of four crown classes of trees. The tree that receive full sunlight from above, but little from the sides.
COMPARTMENT = a forest subdivision used for adminstrative purposes. It has clearly identifiable boundaries and is permanent.
CONK = the fruiting body of a wood-destroying fungus.
COPPICE = a silvicultural cutting method that relies on sprouting for reproduction.
COVER TYPE (FOREST COVER TYPE) = a stand of trees defined by the species composition.
CULL LOG = a log that is rejected because it does not meet specifications.
CUTOVER = an area that has been recently logged, usually by clearcutting.
DAMPING-OFF = the rotting of seedlings soon after emergence due to fungi.
DEADMAN = an anchor (buried log etc.) to hold a guy rope or cable.
DECK = a pile or stack of logs.
DENDROLOGY = the science of tree identification.
DEPLETION ALLOWANCE = a deduction from taxable income at the time of logging to enable recovery of the cash investment (comparable to depreciation but only allowed when logging is done, not yearly).
DIBBLE = a tool used for preparing holes in the ground for tree seedlings.
DOMINANT = one of the four tree-crown classes where the trees get full sunlight from above and partly from the side.
DORMANCY = a condition of a seed or a plant (tree) in which life functions are at a standstill such as in the winter.

DUFF = the layer of fallen leaves, twigs, branches on the forest floor.

EASEMENT = the right of making limited use of another's property such as a right-of-way.

EMINENT DOMAIN = the power to take private property for public use but with compensation.

EVEN-AGED FOREST = a forest comprised of stands of trees where each of the stands are about the same age.

FLUME = a wooden water trough to carry logs or lumber.

FREE-ON-BOARD (f.o.b.) = indicates that the quoted price includes the loading of the goods on the carrier, but not the ensuing transport.

FUNGICIDE = a chemical that kills fungus.

GREEN CHAIN = a long conveyor belt system in a saw mill that conveys and sorts freshly cut lumber.

GYPO (OR GYPPO) = an independent logger, usually a small operator.

HIGH-GRADE = to harvest only the best trees in a stand.

HIGH-LEAD = a cable logging system in which a tall spar tree is used as a tower to lift the front ends of logs as they are skidded.

HOEDAG = a hoe-like hand tool used in tree planting.

INCREMENT = the growth of trees such as the increase in diameter, height, volume, or value.

INTOLERANT = trees that cannot develop and grow normally in the shade of other trees.

KILN = a structure in which lumber is seasoned artificially by heating.

KRAFT PAPERS = high-strength papers made from wood pulp. They can be unbleached used for wrapping or they can be bleached and used for strong bond or book paper.

LANDING = an area of flat ground where logs are collected, sorted and loaded onto trucks or rail cars.

LUMP-SUM TIMBER SALE = a sale where the price is agreed upon prior to logging.

MEAN ANNUAL INCREMENT = the total volume of a stand of trees divided by the age.

MONOCULTURE = repeatedly raising tree crops of a single species.

MYCORRHIZAE = a beneficial fungus that helps roots absorb nutrients.

PATHOGEN = an organism causing disease.

PEAVEY = a hand tool with a spike point and a large hook for moving logs.

PECKERWOOD MILL = a small sawmill that operates intermittently.

PEELER LOG = a log suitable for producing rotary cut veneer.

POLE = a young tree that is between 4" and 12" dbh.

POPPLE = a common name for aspen trees (coming from the Latin name *populus*).

PROVENANCE = geographical origin of tree seed.

SHAKE = a hand-split wooden shingle.
SHAKE BOLT = a block of wood from which shakes are split.
SKIDDER = a machine used to haul logs to the landing.
SKID ROAD = a trail used by the skidder in hauling logs.
SLASH = tops and limbs of trees that are left in the woods after logging.
SNAG = a standing dead tree. Some are valuable to wildlife as a perch or nesting place.
STAND = a group of trees with similar characteristics distinguishable from neighboring stands. A stand is termed a PURE STAND when 80 percent or more of the trees are the same species.
STAND TABLE = table showing the number of trees by species and diameter.
STOCKING = an indication of the number of trees per acre in a stand compared to the ideal.
STRATIFICATION = a cold moist storage period for tree seed (simulates winter).
TAIGA = the coniferous northern forest, shorter trees, more open canopy. the transition zone to tundra.
TOLERANT = trees capable of developing and growing in the shade of other trees.
TRANSPLANT = a tree seedling that has been moved and replanted.
TREE FARM = a trade mark used by the American Forest Institute to designate a privately-owned managed forest.
TSI = timber stand improvement (to improve the condition of a stand but without producing any revenue).
VIGOR = the general health of a tree or stand.
WANE = presence of bark on a corner or edge of lumber.
WATER-BAR = a cross ditch or raised barrier so as to lead the water off a road.
WIDOW-MAKER = a loose limb on a tree which may fall on a logger working beneath it.
WINDROW = a long, narrow pile of slash.
WOLF TREE = a tree that has wide-spreading form and occupies more space than its value permits.
YARD = (see landing) a central point for sorting logs and loading onto trucks.

NOTES

NOTES

NOTES

NOTES

NOTES